AF263222

The Vanishing
Black Family

The Vanishing Black Family

How Welfare and Feminism
Made Marriage Optional and
Children Vulnerable

• • •

Delano Squires

Sentinel

Sentinel
An imprint of Penguin Random House LLC
1745 Broadway, New York, NY 10019
penguinrandomhouse.com

Copyright © 2026 by Delano Squires

Most Sentinel books are available at a discount when purchased in quantity for sales promotions or corporate use. Special editions, which include personalized covers, excerpts, and corporate imprints, can be created when purchased in large quantities. For more information, please call (212) 572-2232 or email specialmarkets@penguinrandomhouse.com. Your local bookstore can also assist with discounted bulk purchases using the Penguin Random House corporate Business-to-Business program. For assistance in locating a participating retailer, email B2B@penguinrandomhouse.com.

Book design by Alissa Rose Theodor

LIBRARY OF CONGRESS CONTROL NUMBER: 2026009858
ISBN 9780593852675 (hardcover)
ISBN 9780593852682 (ebook)

Printed in the United States of America
1st Printing

The authorized representative in the EU for product safety and compliance is Penguin Random House Ireland, Morrison Chambers, 32 Nassau Street, Dublin D02 YH68, Ireland, https://eu-contact.penguin.ie.

*To the children who benefit from the
coming revival of marriage and family*

Contents

Introduction

• • •

Raise your hand if you're married."

This was the opening line in a 1986 CBS documentary on black families in Newark, New Jersey. Bill Moyers, the journalist who narrated the television special, asked this question to about ten young black mothers sitting in a semicircle. None of the women raised their hands. He continued by asking how many of the mothers would like to be married to the father of their child. One hand went up. Moyers asked the others why they didn't plan to get married. The first young woman said she was reluctant to take on the responsibility that comes with caring for a husband in addition to a child. Another stated that she wouldn't want a man holding her down before confidently declaring, "I think I can make it as a single parent." Moyers, clearly seeking to understand the women, asked, "Don't you think you might need help in raising that baby from a man?" The first mother spoke up again, but this time the camera shot also included her baby. The child—who appeared to be a little boy not quite two—looked up at his mother as Moyers asked the question. He was too young to understand his mother's answer, but the viewers certainly could. "Not really," she said. "I didn't have a father." You could see how her experience growing up without a father influenced her ultimate conclusion: "Male figures are not substantially important in the family."[1]

That documentary, *The Vanishing Family: Crisis in Black America*, took an honest look at the breakdown of the traditional family structure in the inner city. Many of the mothers interviewed for the program were on welfare. One of the fathers said that providing for his children was the responsibility of their mothers and the government. According to Moyers,

> In cities all over America the traditional family no longer exists. It has vanished and something new is taking its place. Single women and the children they're rearing alone are the fastest growing part of the black population.[2]

The diminishment of marriage and disappearance of men had already become a reality for many black families by the mid-1980s. The national nonmarital birth rate in the year the documentary was released was 23 percent.[3] For black women, it was 62 percent.[4] If the young mother from Newark is right, these statistics don't suggest a problem. But, if fathers do in fact play an irreplaceable role in the life of a family, what does their absence do to their children?

One of the most memorable television moments of the 1990s steers us toward an answer to the million-dollar question about whether dads really do matter. *The Fresh Prince of Bel-Air* was a popular NBC sitcom that made Will Smith a household name. The show tells the story of how the title character, Will, born and raised in West Philadelphia, got into a fight with some neighborhood bullies that prompted his mother to send him to live with relatives in one of the wealthiest neighborhoods in Los Angeles.

Will has challenges at times going from his working-class background to his new affluent surroundings. His aunt and uncle—Philip "Uncle Phil" and Vivian "Aunt Viv" Banks—are steadying forces in his life, the former being an imposing figure who is stern but loving.

In the episode entitled "Papa's Got a Brand New Excuse," Will's biological father, Lou, comes to see him fourteen years after walking out of his life. Uncle Phil is skeptical of Lou's sudden reappearance but eventually supports the father's offer to take Will on a cross-country trip. Will is excited to spend time with his dad, but Lou shows up on the day of their trip and tells Vivian and Philip that he has to leave town immediately to address an important business matter. Uncle Phil tells Lou he can't keep coming in and out of Will's life, that a father should be present for his children, not keep them waiting on him. Lou doesn't want to hear the lecture and asks him to tell Will their trip is off. After Uncle Phil refuses, Lou says he will call Will to tell him before turning to leave.

But just before Lou rounds the corner and races out the door, Will walks in. Scrambling for an excuse, Lou tells Will that some business has come up and they will need to postpone their trip. Will is visibly disappointed but tries to play it cool. Lou says he'll call his son the following week to reschedule their trip, but Will can sense that his father's promise is empty.

After Lou leaves, Uncle Phil comes to Will's side to comfort him.

Will expresses frustration at wasting money on a present for his dad, which he pulls out of his bag and puts on the table. His voice raises as he recounts all that he'd accomplished without his father, from learning to ride a bike and shoot a basketball to shaving and driving. If he did everything before without his father, he could do the rest—college, marriage, kids—now.

He continues, the emotion building. "I'll be a better father than he ever was, and I sure as hell don't need him for that, cuz ain't a damn thing he could ever teach me about how to love my kids!"

At this point, Will barely holds back tears. Voice quivering, he looks at Uncle Phil and asks the only question that matters at that point: "How come he don't want me, man?"

The tears begin to fall as his uncle engulfs him in an embrace. The scene ends with the camera slowly panning to the gift Will had gotten his father—a hand-carved sculpture of a man holding his son in his lap.[5]

All these years later, it is hard to watch the scene without becoming emotional. The comments under any of the various clips online always include several people who saw their own life story reflected on the screen. They appreciate the powerful acting but also see the deep message. The void created by Lou's abandonment was too large for even Uncle Phil's massive frame to fill. Will's dad was a truck driver who wore work boots, a hoodie, and a knit hat. Uncle Phil was a wealthy lawyer who dressed in suits and cardigans. Nothing the Banks family offered Will—the large home, private school, nice clothes—could satisfy his longing for a father.

These two scenes—one real, the other fictional—paint a picture of black family life that some people would rather ignore. Mothers who don't think men play an important role in the home, dads who come in and out of their children's lives, and kids caught in the middle of a family drama they had no hand in creating. While this certainly does not describe every black family, the reality is that 69 percent of black children today are born to unwed parents.[6] Nearly 45 percent live with a single mother.[7] This means the traditional family—a husband and wife raising their biological children—has given way in far too many neighborhoods to a culture where marriage is obsolete and fathers are optional.

Still, many people don't think this new family structure in black America is a problem. In fact, the politicians, journalists, and academics who talk the most about race never look to the home to explain persistent disparities in social outcomes like poverty and crime. Their long list of root causes includes employment discrimination, education funding, wealth inequality, food deserts, access to healthcare, housing instability, and gentrification. To be clear, this is only a partial list. Progressive politicians—including the black executives who lead some of our largest cities—frequently talk about how political institutions and social structures impact black Americans. And yet they're silent about the institution of marriage and importance of family structure. They claim that complex economic and social forces determine the life trajectory of a little black boy in Brooklyn but somehow believe that the relationship between the parents who created him is irrelevant. When it comes to whether black children excel in the schoolhouse or end up in the jailhouse, they focus far more on the halls of power than the home.

But their blindness does not erase the problem. What Bill Moyers called a crisis in the mid-1980s has turned into a full-blown state of emergency today. The traditional black family has become all but extinct in many communities. What makes the problem even worse is the fact that the separation of marriage and children is no longer confined to poor women in the inner city. The notion that men are expendable and not needed to play the roles of husband and father in the home is promoted and defended by black elites in media and academia.

That needs to change.

Decades of research prove what most people already know: Children raised in homes with their married biological parents do better according to a variety of metrics than children raised in other family arrangements, particularly single-parent homes. The most basic of these is economic stability. Roughly 8 percent of children with married parents live below the poverty line, compared with 35 percent with a single mom.[8] That pattern remains consistent across race. A 2018 federal report found that 45 percent of black children raised by a single mother lived in poverty, compared with 12 percent for those living with married parents.[9]

Single mothers of every background face an elevated risk of poverty, but black mothers and children are particularly vulnerable since the marriage-before-carriage approach to forming a family is now the exception, not the norm. Progressives talk a lot about racial disparities in household income but never seem to include family structure in their calculations. For instance, median household income figures by race follow the same order as marriage rates. Among adults who are 18 and over, 62 percent of Asians, 53 percent of whites, 47 percent of Hispanics, and 35 percent of blacks are married.[10] It is no surprise then that Asians have the highest earnings ($121,700), followed by whites ($92,530), Hispanics ($70,950), and then blacks ($56,020).[11] The median income for black married couples under 65 ($121,900), however, is higher than the overall household income for all groups.[12] By contrast, the median household income for single black women is $50,720.[13]

These statistics should never be used to demean single mothers who work tirelessly to provide for their children. They are simply a reminder that neither the blessings nor the burdens of raising a child are meant for one parent alone.

Children living with their married birth parents also earn better grades and are less likely to be suspended or expelled from school than those in single-parent homes.[14] Likewise, married parents are less likely to be contacted about disruptive behavior, and their children are less likely to be held back.[15] Children in nuclear families have higher rates of college enrollment and lower rates of incarceration as adults.[16] Adolescent girls with present and involved fathers are less likely to engage in risky sexual behaviors and become teenage mothers.[17]

No matter the metric, the evidence is clear: A world in which every black child was raised in a loving household with a married mom and dad would do far more to advance racial equality than a new government program or social justice campaign. Marriage matters because families matter, and families matter because children matter.

There is no question that rebuilding the black family is a worthy cause. You cannot have a strong, thriving nation without strong communities. You cannot have strong communities without strong families. And you cannot have strong families without strong marriages. In many ways, the destruction of marriage is the real root cause of the social ills plaguing many black neighborhoods, not the long list provided by progressives. But it's important to assess how the structure collapsed before beginning a massive renovation project. When the political left periodically acknowledges the breakdown of the family, it most commonly blames the current state of affairs on the legacy of slavery and mass incarceration. Others will add in deindustrialization and redlining. While these views are understandable, they miss the true nature of the issue.

Every trend related to the family involves at least one of three fundamental elements: men, women, and the institution of marriage. Any analysis of the rise in fractured families must deal with the systemic, societal, and fundamental threats to at least one of those three. Yet this is where the progressive narrative falls apart. For example, economic instability explains why a man may not feel ready for a family, but it does not explain why he would have a child—or multiple children—with a woman he refuses to marry. Wage stagnation also doesn't explain why a sharecropper in the

Deep South at the turn of the twentieth century was more likely to be married to the mother of his five children than a professional basketball player earning $40 million per year.

Am I saying the plight of the black family is not mainly an economic problem? Yes, that is exactly what I am saying. The traditional family structure has been replaced by the single-mother model because men and women no longer believe marriage is *valuable, desirable, accessible, and indispensable* for the purpose of starting a family. Put another way, a black child born to—and raised by—their married mother and father under the same roof through their eighteenth birthday is the exception because people no longer want it to be the norm.

There are only two responses to this reality. The first is to accept the current state of the black family as the result of complex social, political, and economic forces interacting in ways that are impossible to change. This response consigns more black children to poverty, crime, delinquency, and academic underachievement. Even those who succeed by these metrics will still be left with that painful existential question: "How come he don't want me, man?" The second is to pursue the hard work of rebuilding the family, a multi-generational project that requires a cultural commitment to reviving the institution of marriage. Beyond its connection to improved social outcomes, this response will provide more black children with the ultimate privilege: growing up in a loving, stable, and secure home with a married mother and father.

I saw the effects of the second option play out in my own life. As a teenager growing up in New York City, I often wondered why my life and the lives of my friends looked so different from some of our less fortunate peers. It certainly wasn't money. Our parents were not rich by any stretch. The difference is that all of us grew up in homes with parents committed to each other in marriage who raised us according to their Christian faith. Each of us grew up with a father in the home as well as a community of men who took their roles as providers, protectors, and role models seriously. The spiritual foundation our parents laid down in our youth explains why I believe a *biblical* blueprint is needed to rebuild the black family.

So yes, I am a Christian, husband, and father—in that order and before anything else. But I'm also a black man with a deep appreciation for the template created by African American leaders in past generations. That includes Booker T. Washington's focus on building and maintaining institutions as well as the moral clarity and conviction of Frederick Douglass. These men are often characterized as "conservative" in debates about race and politics, but like them, my conservatism is far more concerned with the pursuit of human flourishing in the family, community, and nation than with electoral politics. My work today as a researcher focused on marriage and family reflects these priorities.

While I have been formally researching marriage and family for more than a decade, I devoted myself to the issue much earlier. In 2010, I began writing for a website, created by Lamar and Ronnie Tyler, called Black and Married with Kids (BMWK). I offered up practical advice on dating—as a single man—and sparked important conversations on the family that were reflected in titles such as "5 Things Every Man Needs to Learn Before He Gets Married" and "Some Men Still Do Care About Love and Fatherhood." Not only did BMWK give me my start as a writer, it also is the reason I am a husband and father today. I met my wife Stephanie in 2011 at a movie theater in Washington, DC, where the Tylers were premiering their third documentary. We married a year later.

This combination of personal experience, professional expertise, and public advocacy are what brought me to this moment and inspired me to write this book.

The first half of *The Vanishing Black Family* deals directly with the factors that have made marriage optional and children vulnerable. I begin with the legacy of slavery and explain how the black family survived centuries of racial hostility but began to disintegrate after welfare and feminism created division in the home. The first half of the book also examines how black leaders allowed the culture of broken homes to spread and explains why progressive pastors obsessed with politics refuse to affirm biblical teachings on sex, marriage, and family. There is a short interlude before the second half of the book that calls for a new era of back family life dedicated to reviving marriage and rebuilding the home. The second half of the book provides a blueprint for family restoration that reframes the issue to focus on the rights of children, outlines the role of important cultural institutions, and prepares family advocates for criticism from self-professed "allies" of black America. The book ends with a call to action for anyone committed to the hard work of reviving marriage and rebuilding the black family.

Thankfully, I am far from the only one who wants to end the injustice millions of black children are forced to endure when marriage becomes obsolete and fathers are seen as optional in the home. More people are waking up to the truth and know that it is *impossible* for any group of people to thrive without strong families. They share my desire to see the restoration of the traditional family structure in black America and want every child to be born into a home with a father and mother who have committed to each other as husband and wife. They want the marriage and family culture that began to unravel in the 1960s but don't know what must be done today to restore it.

This book is their answer.

The Vanishing
Black Family

ONE

Slavery and the Black Family

A Story of Resistance and Survival

One of the bravest acts any slave could attempt was an escape to freedom. What seems like an easy decision to people who know only a life of individual liberty and personal autonomy was far more complicated for slaves who knew that being captured meant both a return to their previous condition and the prospect of severe punishment. Whipping was common. Some slaves were branded and others chained to prevent further attempts at escape. And in some cases, runaways who were caught faced dismemberment or the ultimate penalty: death. Harsh punishments were meant to dissuade slaves from attempting subsequent escapes and to serve as a hedge against social contagion.

Such cruelties were supported by both law and custom. The Fugitive Slave Act of 1793 enforced the Fugitive Slave Clause in the US Constitution that required captured slaves in other states to be returned to their owners.[1] Put simply, any slave contemplating escape understood the stakes, and those who did run away decided that living as a free person was worth the risk.

Married couples had the most to lose. They knew that physical punishment was all but guaranteed if they were captured, but permanent separation from a spouse and children would also leave life-long emotional scars. The prospect of being torn from one's family and sold to another owner hundreds of miles away was a good reason to *not* attempt an escape. But for some, the idea of enjoying the full benefits of marriage was the ultimate motivation for pursuing freedom.

Those who were willing to risk life, limb, and liberty for the sake of love put slavery's impact on the black family—both then and now—in its proper perspective. Slavery undoubtedly deformed the institution of marriage and distorted relationships between the men and women whose unions lacked both social recognition and legal protection. It did not *destroy* the black family, however, because of the courage and persistence displayed over centuries by both slaves and freedmen alike.

There are countless stories in the historical record of enslaved couples who fought to form and preserve families. One of the most compelling examples of resistance and resilience is the daring escape of William and Ellen Craft. The Crafts, who were both born into slavery, lived in Macon, GA, and were owned by different masters. Ellen had very light skin and was frequently mistaken for white due to being the child of her master and one of his biracial slaves. William was a cabinetmaker who was sold as a teenager to help settle his master's debts.[2] They knew each other for years before making plans to build a family together, but they postponed their marriage because the law at the time required children born to slave mothers to inherit the same condition.[3] Ellen and William eventually married, but their experience with brutal family separations filled them with fear that the same would happen to their future children.[4] So the Crafts hatched a plan to gain their freedom. They didn't flee on foot or on horseback in the dead of night. They chose an even riskier method of escape: hiding in plain sight by having Ellen dress as a young white planter and William her slave.

There was a catch, however. It was not common for women to travel alone with male servants, so Ellen had to pose as a man. William cut Ellen's hair and she dressed in a pair of men's trousers that she sewed herself.[5] She put her right arm in a sling to dissuade authorities from expecting her to sign any documents. This detail served far more than an aesthetic purpose. Neither Craft could read or write due to a Georgia law that prohibited teaching slaves to do either. William also wrapped bandages around much of Ellen's face to give her a reason to avoid speaking with strangers. A top hat and pair of green spectacles completed the transformation.[6]

With that, the couple set their plan in motion. On December 21, 1848, Ellen, dressed as young white male slave owner, boarded a train from Macon to Savannah with William posing as "his" servant. As was the custom at the time, William sat in the "Negro car" while his wife rested quietly in another part of the train.[7] The couple's ruse could have ended just as abruptly as it began after William spotted the owner of the cabinetmaking shop looking through the windows of each car. William turned and sank down into his seat, preparing for the worst, but the train pulled off just before the man reached his car.[8]

The pair arrived in Savannah and boarded a steamship to Charleston, South Carolina. The captain of the vessel complimented the young planter on the attentiveness of his slave and warned the seemingly injured owner about "cut-throat abolitionists" in the North who would encourage William to run away and seek his freedom.[9] This wasn't the only time William garnered attention during this journey. A slave trader on board inquired about purchasing him, but his wife-turned-master refused the offer. The pair attempted to buy tickets from South Carolina to Philadelphia but encountered another hurdle. The young planter was required to sign documents proving he owned William—a policy instated to prevent white abolitionists from taking slaves out of the South. The ticket seller refused to bend the rules even though the owner's arm was in a sling, but the captain vouched for the pair and signed their names.[10]

Baltimore was the last major stop before the Crafts reached the free state of Pennsylvania. The authorities there were particularly vigilant. The couple was asked to leave the train for verification of ownership. An officer told them they were being detained.[11] The couple prayed silently while contemplating the prospect of being returned to slavery. They knew what would happen if they were caught. A brutal whipping was all but guaranteed. Their masters could have also sold them to different plantations hundreds of miles away as final punishment for their act of rebellion. Their dream of building a family together in freedom was on the verge of turning into their worst nightmare.[12]

Then the departure bell shattered the quiet.

The border patrol officer, agitated but needing to act decisively, looked at the planter—with his bandaged face and arm immobilized in a sling—and sent word to the conductor: "Let this gentleman and slave pass."[13]

On Christmas day, William and Ellen arrived in Philadelphia, where they were given assistance and housing by a local abolitionist group.[14] They also received a reading lesson their first day in the city. The Crafts left for Boston a few weeks later, where William found work as a cabinetmaker and Ellen became a seamstress. Unfortunately, this was not their final move. Congress passed the Fugitive Slave Act in 1850, and slave hunters attempted to apprehend them in Boston and take them back to Georgia. The Crafts fled the country for England, where they had five children—all born in freedom.[15] The couple eventually returned to Georgia in 1870 and opened the Woodville Co-operative Farm School three years later for the education and employment of newly freed men and women.[16]

William and Ellen Craft's great escape is a testament to the lengths people will go for love—and freedom. Their story also challenges the idea that African American family dynamics today are a direct result of slavery.

This flawed idea is so persuasive because it contains a kernel of truth: Slavery *did* affect every aspect of black family life—a fact demonstrated by the Crafts' story and others like it. But the couple's ultimate triumph also points to something else: Assessing slavery's connection to contemporary black family life is mainly an ideological battle over *narratives,* not facts.

Liberals tie the breakdown of the family today to chattel slavery by arguing that the racist nature of the institution was resurrected and reinstituted through Jim Crow segregation, the war on drugs, and mass incarceration. They see a common theme at play, namely structural barriers that limit economic opportunity or remove black men from their homes. For people on the political left, slavery's effect on the black family—even in the story of William and Ellen Craft—is about the actions of hostile oppressors.

Conservatives take a different perspective. For them, the most noteworthy takeaway from the Craft's daring escape is the couple's courage, not the fact that slavery existed and frequently tore families apart. To people on the political right, any connection between slavery and the condition of the black family since the 1960s is based on parallels they observe between the welfare state and the "benevolent" paternalism of slave owners whose willingness to provide food, clothes, and shelter for their subjects was one example of the control they exerted over them.

Both sides make valid arguments, but there is far more at stake in their ongoing debate than historical accuracy. Narratives shape how people see the past, interpret the present, and plan for the future. When the horrors of slavery become the central theme of the black family, the stories we tell about that era will focus on the actions of the villains (i.e., slave owners who broke up homes) rather than the heroes (i.e., couples who fought for their families). That approach will inevitably lead to calls for white people *today* to "fix" the black family, a phenomenon that is already seen in public discourse on racial disparities in education, criminal justice, and other important social outcomes. This is the path that consigns blacks in America to supporting roles in our own autobiography.

There is another approach that is far more powerful—and useful—for a movement dedicated to rebuilding the black family. It includes an honest account of the role slavery played in erecting legal, political, and social impediments to marriage. But it emphasizes the strength and resolve of the men and women who formed families together despite those obstacles. Why? Because the stories of men and women who married and had children under the yoke of bondage contain valuable lessons about hope, love, sacrifice, and dedication for those who have the privilege of forming families in freedom. This knowledge of what is possible when two people dedicate themselves to building a future together—despite their family histories, their social standing, and the political climate—is exactly what is needed to spark the movement needed to rebuild the black family *today*.

Slavery and the War on Wedlock

The starting point for an honest historical analysis of the black family must begin with the acknowledgement that slavery and marriage are completely incompatible institutions that cannot coexist. Marriage creates a bond between a husband and wife, reflected in the biblical belief that the "two become one" in their union. Those bonds strengthen after children are born. This family structure is the bedrock of society, but a slave owner could sever the bonds between a husband and wife at any time. Slavery had a similarly destructive effect on the relationship between parents and their children. In many respects the "black family" itself was a declaration of independence from the complete control slave owners sought to exert over their "property."

The legal theory that slaves were property predated the nation's founding. Daniel Dulany, an influential lawyer in Maryland, issued an opinion in 1767 involving manumitted slaves. In it, he stated, "either the master's property must give way for the support of the marriage of a female slave, or her marriage must be deemed invalid in order to preserve her master's property."[17] This view was the foundation for denying slaves legal marital rights for most of the nineteenth century.

Dred Scott v. Sandford, a landmark 7–2 US Supreme Court ruling in 1857, concluded that people of African descent were not—and never intended to be—citizens under the Constitution. The Court's majority opinion, written by Chief Justice Roger Taney, held that blacks "had no rights which the white man was bound to respect."[18] The Court's decision also struck down the Missouri Compromise and prohibited the federal government from freeing slaves brought into federal territories. The case is infamous for intensifying contemporary debates on the issue of slavery leading up to the Civil War. What fewer people know is the integral part marriage played in this case: It made a real marriage between slaves legally impossible.

Dred Scott married Harriet Robinson at some point between

1836 and 1837 in a public ceremony that took place in present-day Minnesota, then a federal territory where slavery was prohibited. The ceremony was conducted by Major Lawrence Taliaferro, the bride's master, with the consent of Mr. Scott's master. The couple had their first child, Eliza, in 1838 in free territory.[19] On April 6, 1846, the Scotts filed separate petitions in St. Louis circuit court to obtain their freedom from slavery on the grounds that they lived—and married—in territory where Congress had prohibited slavery.

Scott's case eventually made it to the nation's highest court. The unfavorable outcome of Scott's case is well-known, but few today are aware that one of the judges on the bench, Justice Benjamin R. Curtis, issued a dissenting opinion that, had his reasoning carried the day, would have freed Scott. Curtis cited Scott's marriage as evidence of the masters' intentions to free their slaves.

> In my judgment, there can be no more effectual abandonment of the legal rights of a master over his slave, than by the consent of the master that the slave should enter into a contract of marriage, in a free State, attended by all the civil rights and obligations which belong to that condition.[20]

This line of argument was ultimately rejected. The Court's ruling meant that slaves could marry by their mutual agreement, but their marriages had no legal protections because *they*—the men and women desiring to wed—could not enter into contracts of any kind.

Princeton history professor Tera W. Hunter is the author of *Bound in Wedlock*, a book on black family life during the time of slavery. She reaches a similar conclusion as she captures the incompatibility of the "peculiar institution" of slavery and the institution of marriage perfectly when she states, "slave marriage was superfluous because slaves were already married, symbolically, to their masters."[21]

The basic expectations of a marriage, in principle, include mutual consent, sexual exclusivity, cohabitation, procreation, and permanence.

Slavery, as practiced in the United States, made the fulfillment of basic marital duties and obligations impossible. The movement, labor, material needs, and associations of slaves were all under the control of an owner who had the legal right to buy and sell them at any time, for any reason he chose. A slave owner could separate a married couple, selling one spouse hundreds of miles away from the other. In fact, an estimated one third of first marriages were disrupted by the interstate slave trade.[22] Slaves were often sent away as wedding gifts when the younger relatives of large planters married.[23]

Forced separation is the most vivid example of slavery's impact on marital cohabitation, but it wasn't the only one. Slave couples who were owned by different masters frequently remained on their respective plantations after marrying.[24] These "abroad" marriages undoubtedly impacted their ability to create the types of intimate emotional and sexual bonds that strengthen a marriage. That does not mean couples ignored their marital obligations. Indeed, couples often went to great lengths to preserve their marriages. Husbands typically traveled on weekends and holidays to see their wives, walking several miles each way.[25] They had to secure passes from their owners that gave them permission to be out on the roads in the event they encountered slave patrols.[26]

Tragically, even sexual exclusivity wasn't guaranteed for enslaved couples, who worried about the sexual intrusion of the slave owners and their family members. Some slaves did not want the minister who married them to include the promise of fidelity in their vows because, "at any time our masters could compel us to break such a promise."[27] Sexual exclusivity is one of the most important expectations in any marriage. The fact that it could not be guaranteed due to factors outside the control of enslaved couples had a profound impact on the dynamics between husbands and wives. A married master who had sex with his female slave against her will violated her right to bodily autonomy. He also emasculated her husband, who was unable to protect her either because he lived apart from his wife or feared the consequences of physically intervening. The slave owner also contributed to "illegitimacy" in the event a child was conceived and created a de facto single-mother home if the woman lived apart from her husband.

Slavery made it extremely difficult for husbands to protect their wives and children, but that does not mean men stood idly by in the face of abuse. Their presence on the plantation may have served as a deterrent to sexually opportunistic masters, given the connection between the prevalence of abroad marriages and the higher numbers of biracial slaves in some locations.[28] Other husbands were willing to do more than serve as a passive deterrent to lecherous slave owners. A free black husband was convicted in 1834 of stealing his slave wife from her owner in Delaware.[29] A husband referred to in court documents as only "Alfred (a slave)" was sentenced to death in 1859 for killing an overseer who raped his wife.[30] In other cases that are hard for the modern mind to comprehend, some free black men were willing to consign themselves to slavery if it meant keeping their families intact. One slave owner who submitted a petition on behalf of a free man requesting to become his slave described how the man preferred to be owned by a master of his choice if it meant being together with his wife and children.[31]

Firsthand accounts from former slaves paint a picture of human beings deeply desirous of affection and companionship, despite the obvious barriers slavery placed in the way of marriage. Fulfilling those desires began with the courtship process. Men and women looked for mates in everyday work and leisure activities. The sexes also intermingled at weekend "frolics" where singing and dancing accompanied courtship.[32] The coupling process seemed to follow conventional gender scripts, with men initially expressing interest. Women had the added burden of getting their masters to consent to their desire for marriage. Young women who were interested in a partner the owner did not approve of would be told to make a different choice or be forced to marry someone of his choosing.[33] Couples also sought the approval of their parents, with the marriage ceremony often following shortly after the necessary permissions were secured.[34]

Most slave weddings were modest affairs, an unsurprising reality for people attempting to build marital bonds while in a state of bondage. Although the Bible influenced the social and cultural norms around marriage in the antebellum South, Christian marriages were not the norm for slaves.[35] Slaves who did want a Christian ceremony did not always receive one because owners were reluctant to prioritize the biblical template for husbands and wives over their personal and financial interests.[36] Some slaves were pronounced husband and wife by an owner conducting the ceremony, and the vows recited during the wedding were altered at times to account for the couple's enslaved status. For example, the phrase "till death do you part" was changed in some ceremonies to "until death or distance do you part."[37] Another version—"till death or buckra part you"—included the term slaves used for their white owners and their role as the final authority in a slave couple's marriage.[38] The most common ritual during the ceremony was "jumping the broom," a practice that involved the couple hopping over a broomstick while holding hands to signify starting a new life together. More privileged slaves could have more elaborate ceremonies, including wedding attire and a large feast, but this was far from the norm.

While some slaves embraced marriage despite their lack of autonomy, the low regard their owners and other whites had for their relationships caused some blacks to devalue the institution as well.[39] Some viewed marriage in very pragmatic terms, devoid of emotional sentiment. For them, marriage was a "practical surrender to the need for companionship, domestic help, or a way of escaping from frustrating isolation."[40] Others saw slavery and marriage as opposing forces and did not believe they could inhabit both at the same time.[41] This is what made William and Ellen Craft initially postpone their nuptials and ultimately embark on a risky escape to secure freedom for themselves and their future children.[42]

The Pain of Separation and the Joy of Reunion

Though the institution of slavery posed serious challenges to the couples in its grip, it cannot be understated how much enslaved couples valued marriage. Among the clearest signs of their devotion was how far they were willing to go—sometimes literally—to locate a spouse after gaining their freedom. The Last Seen Project has identified, digitized, transcribed, and published more than 3,500 ads from across the United States by former slaves searching for spouses and family members after emancipation. Drawn from more than 250 newspapers, these ads demonstrate a level of commitment and endurance that prove not even time, distance, or hardship can extinguish the fires of affection that burn deep within the human heart.

One ad in the *Richmond Daily Dispatch* tells the story of Robert

Cox, a slave in Virginia who was sold to a new owner in Georgia months after marrying his wife, who was also sold to someone in another state. Eventually they set out in search of one another, but Cox could not find his wife "after long years of search throughout several of the southern States."[43] Eventually both returned to their old home in Virginia—each unbeknownst to the other—after giving up any hope of reunion. Here is how the paper described the moment they reconnected after twenty-four years:

> When her husband came back again to the old cabin, and he beheld the one he had spent years of sorrow and toil endeavoring to find, they recognized one another, and the shout that arose from that cabin and rang through the forest near by will be remembered by them as long as they live. After finding his wife he carried her down to Georgia to live, and they are at present residing in that State.[44]

Some of the ads included not only a recounting of reunited couples but also social commentary on the reason for their separation. An 1880 ad in the *Cincinnati Enquirer* begins with an important piece of historical context, namely that marriage laws did not apply to blacks in 1857 when the "baneful curse of slavery existed in the South."[45]

The ad goes on to recount Harrison Bradley's marriage to his first wife in 1857 and their subsequent separation on the auction block two years later.[46] Mr. Bradley settled in Ohio after slavery was abolished and, presuming his first wife was deceased, married a second time. The newspaper ad states that his first wife came to his town "by accident" at some point after his second wife died and the two reconnected after not seeing each other for twenty-one years.[47] The couple quickly remarried in the presence of friends—both black and white—and the paper ended its account of their love story this way:

> It is hoped that the aged couple, after so many years of hardships and separation, may yet live a long, happy and prosperous life.[48]

The pain of separation and joy of reunion are common themes in these accounts. Given the fact that the average life expectancy at the turn of the twentieth century was forty-seven years, some couples were forced apart for nearly an entire lifetime before reuniting. The *Davenport Sunday Democrat* announced that the union between "Uncle" Robert Warren and Charity Atwater was solemnized on June 5, 1897, fifty-three years after they had been separated.[49] The ad said the two were married in North Carolina in the 1830s according to slave laws in that state.[50] The couple had five children together, but the husband was sold to another owner in Tennessee, more than 700 miles away.[51] The octogenarian couple eventually reunited and wed, sixty years after they first married.

One weekly paper in Ohio announced the reunification and wedding plans for Aunt Vina Johnson and her husband George Perry, who had been separated for forty-three years.[52] Unlike similar accounts, this couple and their family were torn apart when the husband tried to rescue his wife and child from bondage. His wife's enslaver, identified only as Mr. Johnson, was able to capture Vina and her child. She remained in slavery for an additional thirty years.[53] Mr. Perry eventually located his wife. *The Highland Weekly News* captured the tenderness of their reunion, an important acknowledgement for people who were stripped of legal protections and the presumption of humanity during slavery:

That Aunt Vina was all anxiety and in a fever of excitement no one need be told. True to his promise, Perry arrived on Monday evening, and the meeting was a joyous one. They have determined to be remarried, and are making every preparation for that event.[54]

The presumption of death, and subsequent remarriage, among married slaves was so common that there is an entire series of ads describing the plight of several "Enoch Ardens." That term refers to the Enoch Arden law, a legal doctrine that allows one spouse to remarry if the other has been missing without any explanation after a certain number of years, typically seven.[55] After the required number of years, the missing spouse is declared dead, clearing the path for the living spouse to remarry. The name for this doctrine comes from a British poem about a man named Enoch Arden who goes to sea to provide for his wife and three children.[56] He is shipwrecked on an island, leaving his wife to grieve after he is presumed dead. She remarries after more than a decade and has a child with her new husband. Enoch eventually returns to England and learns that his wife has a new husband and child. He never tells her he is alive and eventually dies, heartbroken that he never again felt the loving embrace of his wife or children.

Unlike the tragic tale of this fictional character, the real-life Enoch Ardens referenced in several newspaper ads did not keep their deep desire for reunification a secret. Not only did men go in search of their wives, but some successfully persuaded them to leave their new husbands. One ad in the *Alexandria Gazette* tells of a man who approached his former wife and her new husband at the wharf as they waited to take a trip to Washington, DC. The woman's husband at the time begged her not to speak to her former spouse, who the paper referred to as a "Bad Enoch Arden," a perspective the woman clearly did not share:

> . . . but the old love was too strong for her to resist its influence, and as she joyously rushed into the arms of number one, number two put his umbrella over his shoulder and deliberately walked off up the street, leaving her alone with him whose smiles first made her weep.[57]

Another ad from 1885 in the *St. Louis Globe-Democrat* tells of "a colored Mrs. Enoch Arden" who was separated from her husband after she and their children were sold to another owner.[58] The man remarried after not hearing from his wife for years and lived with a new wife who was "willing to share the joys and sorrows of his declining years."[59] The first wife eventually located him and asked to meet—a request the second wife supported. The man reunited with his first wife, whom he had not seen in nearly thirty years, and learned that his children were all married and doing well.[60] The ad concludes by stating that the man was now torn between the two women, not knowing which of his wives he should choose.

These ads demonstrated that former slaves believed in marriage and were willing to do everything in their power to fight for their families. They were considered property and denied the legal and social recognition of their unions, yet those obstacles could not disrupt the deepest of human needs. The desire for love and companionship is evident in the narrative accounts of marriages involving both slaves and freedmen. Their resilience reflected the enduring nature of the institution itself.

As is the case with any group of people, the experiences of ex-slaves were not universal. Many chose to formalize their existing relationships, in part due to pressure from family members and clergy.[61] Others continued in informal marriage arrangements where couples lived together, shared finances, and practiced sexual exclusivity without legally marrying.[62] Some families, however, stayed separated, whether for economic reasons or because of their conflicting visions of what it meant to be married as free people.[63] In addition, couples who lived apart during slavery had to adjust to living under a single roof. Women who had grown used to their independence had to learn to live with husbands desiring to lead the household. Likewise, men who were used to living apart from their family had to establish a new norm that included a wife and children.[64]

Like all couples, former slaves had to navigate the complementary roles husbands and wives played in their homes. Marriage gave them a foundation "to gain control over their own labor, acquire the benefits of their own exertions, and protect the physical bodies of kin."[65] Couples were not just supported by family, friends, community, and church. The government also played a role in trying to repair some of the damage slavery inflicted on the black family. The Bureau of Refugees, Freedmen, and Abandoned Lands, also known as the Freedmen's Bureau, was an important institution during the Reconstruction period following the Civil War. It was established by an act of Congress on March 3, 1865, and it mainly dealt with providing food, shelter, and clothing to newly freed black Americans. The Freedmen's Bureau also helped benevolent societies establish schools and managed confiscated or abandoned lands.[66] One of the Bureau's less discussed roles, however, was in facilitating the reconstruction of black families.

A missionary named Mansfield French was appointed supervisor of Missions and Marriage Relations by the Freedmen's Bureau in South Carolina. He wrote a detailed set of rules to regulate the domestic relations of former slaves to, "correct as far as possible one of the most cruel wrongs inflicted by slavery."[67] The goal of the Bureau's postwar family activities was to "establish marriage as a permanent, monogamous, exclusive relationship with husbands assuming power and authority for the care of their wives and children."[68] The marriage rules and laws that were developed during Reconstruction were designed to encourage monogamy by punishing sexual infractions such as adultery, bigamy, domestic violence, and desertion.[69] In addition to moral instruction, Bureau agents helped former slaves find loved ones and provided transportation to freedmen attempting to reunite with their family members. They also helped legalize marriages that began in slavery, settled marital disputes, and worked with state officials to extend marriage protections to former slaves.[70] The government's interest in promoting marriage and adjudicating marital conflicts among blacks during Reconstruction stood in stark contrast to the laws that legalized slavery and wreaked havoc on the black family for more than two hundred years.

Conclusion

Slavery left an indelible imprint on the black family. The incompatibility of the two institutions—slavery and marriage—was seen in everything from courtship to marital cohabitation. Slavery cast a long shadow over the social norms governing the formation of black families—both in bondage and freedom. Many slaves valued marriage and had a deep desire for love, companionship, and family. Others were more ambivalent about the institution, especially when its most basic duties and obligations were threatened by slave owners and denied basic legal protections. Both enslaved men and women had been forced into relationships against their will, with some masters more concerned about breeding healthy slaves than facilitating genuinely loving connections. Having a one-flesh union was nearly impossible when the specter of separation or sexual coercion hung over the marriage.

In the centuries-long fight between the two competing institutions, marriage won, but not without the black family suffering serious wounds. The former slaves who used every resource at their disposal to locate loved ones are a testament to the strength of the human spirit. Still, the black family culture that emerged after two centuries of slavery was characterized by contradiction and complexity. In the heart of the Jim Crow era from 1890 through 1950, black men and women married at younger ages and were more likely to be married by the age of thirty-five than their white counterparts.[71] But African Americans in the early part of the twentieth century also displayed greater signs of family fragility than their white peers. Between 1930 and 1934, 31 percent of first births to black women between fifteen and twenty-nine years old involved unmarried mothers, compared with only 6 percent of white women. Despite all these challenges, black families in the early twentieth century were still largely intact, predominantly due to cultural institutions that promoted marriage.

No institution was more important than the church, which explains why the moral foundation and cultural ethos of the black community during that time was distinctly Christian.

Reverend E. C. Morris was born to slaves in 1855 and eventually rose to become president of the National Baptist Convention. His writing on "Negro" moral life included an important observation about how cultural norms at the time encouraged marriage and discouraged divorce.

The matter of divorce has been a great problem to many of the most thoughtful men of the race, and the frequent resort to the courts to obtain divorces has been used as an argument against the growth of the moral sentiment in the race. But the very fact that such meets with opposition and is disapproved by the good people is evidence in favor of the Negro's morals. Then again, the class of Negroes who have but little respect for the marriage vow are, as a rule, those who are indolent, worthless and without a home and making no effort to obtain one. But, happily, this class form but a small minority.[72]

Use of the terms "indolent" and "worthless" sounds harsh to modern ears, but Rev. Morris, like most black leaders in the early twentieth century, regularly spoke with this type of moral clarity. These leaders understood that the key to stopping a dysfunctional minority within a community from becoming the dominant majority was to address their harmful ideas, values, and behaviors quickly—and firmly—to prevent them from spreading.

Unfortunately, these harmful ideas soon won out. What these leaders feared two generations after the Civil War became reality one generation after the civil rights movement.

Uplift cannot be outsourced. The slaves who endured the most unspeakable evils of that "peculiar institution" knew that. *They* set about trying to find spouses, parents, and children after gaining their freedom. Their descendants—beneficiaries of the sacrifices previous generations made—have no excuse for not doing everything in their power to fight just as hard to restore the institution of marriage. Putting slavery's impact on the development of the black family in proper perspective is essential to understanding the forces that ultimately decimated the home decades later.

While slavery was the most direct assault on the black family, it was not the most effective. The human instinct in response to an attack on something—or someone—you love is to fight. The worst way to gain access to a family's home is attempting to break down the door. Doing so would awaken a husband and make him grab a weapon to defend his wife and children.

A far better way to get inside a family's home is to come offering "help," especially if they trust the person at the door. This is exactly what happened in the 1960s. The proponents of big government liberalism and second-wave feminism made black people enticing offers of financial support and female liberation. The men and women allowed the people bearing these "gifts" into the home, a decision that ultimately destabilized gender roles and decimated the traditional family structure for decades to come.

• • •

PART 1

The Path
to Destruction

TWO

Displace Men
with Welfare

The Washington Post published an article in 2024 that began with a twenty-seven-year-old "stay-at-home mom" in the nation's capital. The woman faced financial hardship just after having had her third child, but fortunately she had a man who took his role as provider very seriously. He paid for the family's two-bedroom apartment in the Anacostia neighborhood and ensured the children had enough to eat while their mother stayed at home. It was hard for the family to get through the month without mom working, but then they received what felt "like a stroke of good fortune." Thanks to the man of the house, their bank account got an extra $10,800 to help with whatever they wanted—bills, clothes, even a vacation.[1]

The phrase "stay-at-home mom" typically implies that a man—most often a woman's husband—is working to provide for his family so she can focus on raising their children. Its use in the *Washington Post* story was perfectly consistent with that framework, except for one key difference: The "man" providing for the material needs of the mother was Uncle Sam.

With Temporary Assistance for Needy Families (TANF) as her

only income, the mother of three paid $120 a month in rent for her subsidized two-bedroom apartment. Food stamps and WIC, a program that offers nutritional support for low-income mothers, helped cover the groceries. And that $10,800 a year? It was a direct cash assistance pilot program from the DC government that provided the funds either as a lump sum or monthly payment. One of only two times the word "father" is used in the entire *Post* article is when "the children's father" joined them on a $6,000 family trip to Florida after mom took a lump sum payout from Uncle Sam. (The other instance was when another woman mentioned that the fathers of her seventeen-year-old and one-year-old "have been in and out of their lives.")[2]

American family life has changed a great deal over the past sixty years. Marriage rates are down. Those who do marry are waiting longer than ever to tie the knot. Cohabitation is common, and for many couples, babies are a "yes" while marriage is a "maybe." The share of husbands who are the sole or primary breadwinners decreased from 85 percent in 1972 to 55 percent in 2022, while the number of wives in that role increased from 5 percent to 16 percent during the same period.[3] One thing, however, remains constant: The responsibilities to protect and provide remains the bare minimum society expects from every able-bodied man with a family. Men have played these roles for all of human history. Those who neglect their responsibilities can expect to be shamed and stigmatized. It's not hard to figure out why: No culture teaches women *they* are responsible for providing for an adult male and the children they have together.

The expectation that a man will provide for his household is universal. What has changed isn't that a man must provide. It's *which* man must provide. All of the women in the *Washington Post* story were black, a reflection of an all-too-common reality in poor neighborhoods created in part by the rapid expansion of the welfare state, starting in the 1960s. News stories about black family life that render black men invisible should come as no surprise after decades of bad public policy helped dislodge them from their God-given role as providers and displace them from their homes. The void created by their absence was filled by the government, which led to a transformation of the black family that was predicted in one of the most controversial government reports in American history.

The Moynihan Prophecy

In 1965, Daniel Patrick Moynihan, then Assistant Secretary of Labor under President Lyndon Johnson, released a report that is still being discussed and debated to this day. The Moynihan Report, as it has been called for decades, was formally titled *The Negro Family: The Case for National Action.* Moynihan wrote that in the post-Jim Crow era—punctuated by the passage of the Civil Rights Act of 1964—African Americans would expect equal opportunities to generally produce equal outcomes compared with other groups.[4] He believed that was unlikely to happen, however, for two reasons. The first was another generation of personal prejudice directed at black Americans due to the residual effects of the "racist virus in the American bloodstream." The second, in his words, was that "three centuries of sometimes unimaginable mistreatment" had a profound impact on blacks, leading to individual successes but collective stagnation. Moynihan argued at the time that despite gains in education and income, the "gap between the Negro and most other groups in American society is widening."[5] Nothing made this clearer to Moynihan than the state of the black family, especially in the inner city.

> The fundamental problem, in which this is most clearly the case, is that of family structure. The evidence—not final, but powerfully persuasive—is that the Negro family in the urban ghettos is crumbling. A middle-class group has managed to save itself, but for vast numbers of the unskilled, poorly educated city working class the fabric of conventional social relationships has all but disintegrated. There are indications that the situation may have been arrested in the past few years, but the general post-war trend is unmistakable. So long as this situation persists, the cycle of poverty and disadvantage will continue to repeat itself.[6]

Moynihan pointed to several indicators to justify his concerns about the traditional black family. His report stated that close to one quarter of black women living in cities "who have ever married are divorced, separated, or are living apart from their husbands."[7] He also stated the nonmarital birth rate for blacks rose from 16.8 percent in 1940 to 23.6 percent in 1963. For context, the rate for whites increased from 2 percent to 3.07 percent over the same time period. Moynihan also reported 14 percent of black children were receiving Aid to Families with Dependent Children (AFDC) assistance, compared with only 2 percent of white children. He concluded that the "steady expansion of this welfare program, as of public assistance programs in general, can be taken as a measure of the steady disintegration of the Negro family structure over the past generation in the United States."[8] Moynihan saw early signs that black family life was beginning to unravel and viewed welfare dependency as a symptom of family breakdown.

He cited several explanations for what he observed at the time, none of which included any form of blood-and-bone biological deficiency. Writing a hundred years after the Emancipation Proclamation was signed, he believed that slavery played a significant role in the development of the black family structure at the time. He noted the male slave's inability to fulfill his obligations as husband and father, specifically because of the fact that his children could be sold and his wife sexually violated by her owner.[9] Moynihan went on to quote a social psychologist who noted that the prevalence of slave owners separating families meant "the slave household often developed a fatherless matrifocal (mother-centered) pattern."[10]

The role men are meant to play as providers was a recurring theme in Moynihan's report. He noted that *work*, not welfare, was needed for men to fulfill their duty as the heads of households.[11] His report included an analysis of economic data that found the black family was stable when work was plentiful and, conversely, grew more fragile as jobs became more difficult to find.[12] He also found that black men had higher rates of unemployment, lower wages, and larger families compared with their white counterparts, all factors that made it more difficult for them to support their households.

Moynihan was also interested in how gender dynamics played out in the black family. He noted that while workforce participation by black men was higher than for black women, there were certain positions where women made up most of the black workforce. Moynihan noted that 70 percent of the black employees at the Department of Labor, where he was assistant secretary, were women, compared with 42 percent of the white employees.[13] This gender imbalance could also be seen in education, where black women had lower dropout rates and higher college attendance rates than their male counterparts.[14] Moynihan believed that these larger structural factors led to the "reversed roles of husband and wife"—with women replacing men as heads of households—in many black families, a pattern that "reinforces itself over the generations."[15] Moynihan saw this "matriarchal" family structure, especially in cities, as detrimental to the progress of black Americans. Yet, two sentences in his report reflect a worldview that has decimated the traditional black family over the past six decades.

> There is, presumably, no special reason why a society in which males are dominant in family relationships is to be preferred to a matriarchal arrangement. However, it is clearly a disadvantage for a minority group to be operating on one principle, while the great majority of the population, and the one with the most advantages to begin with, is operating on another.[16]

For all his policy credentials, Moynihan's belief that the only issue with the prevalence of a matriarchal structure within black families was the departure from white social norms set the stage for ideas that made the problems he wanted to solve even worse. Foremost among them is the belief that a man's role as provider can be outsourced to the government. Moynihan's subtle concession to the matriarchy was a harbinger of the parallel family structure that became entrenched in low-income black neighborhoods over subsequent generations. The new norm of single mothers raising children with the financial support of the federal government was promoted and defended by both intellectual and political elites for several decades. In the end, the institution that preserved African Americans during the darkest periods in our nation's history was devastated by people whose "help" for black families sent the message that men are optional when Uncle Sam is the man of the house.

A New Patriarch

The Moynihan Report concluded with a declaration that the programs of the federal government should be designed to "enhance the stability and resources of the Negro American family."[17] This call to action came months before President Lyndon B. Johnson's commencement speech at Howard University that included the foundation upon which big government paternalism has rested for more than sixty years.

> You do not take a person who, for years, has been hobbled by chains and liberate him, bring him up to the starting line of a race and then say, "you are free to compete with all the others," and still justly believe that you have been completely fair.[18]

A much lesser-known part of President Johnson's address to the students at Howard was his belief that the family is the "cornerstone" of our society and that broken homes have a devastating effect on their surrounding communities.[19] He acknowledged that men need jobs that help them provide for a family. He also expressed the importance of welfare and social programs that encourage families to stay together. You can see the appeal of this idea in theory. People never want to see families struggle and children suffer because of circumstances outside their control. You can also see a preview of the cultural tug-of-war between black men and the federal government over who would provide for black women and their children. As Moynihan noted, family stability increases when men have jobs that enable them to support their households. The federal government, however, has far more control over how much it spends on welfare and programs for families than it does over finding any specific man steady employment.

It should come as no surprise that the years following the enactment of Johnson's Great Society initiatives brought a significant increase in federal spending meant to fight poverty and help families. In 1950, total federal expenditures on public aid programs, a fraction of total social welfare spending, totaled $1 billion.[20] By 1975, it had ballooned to $27 billion.[21] It reached $62 billion by 1985.[22] The majority of this spending took the form of cash assistance from AFDC, Medicaid, and food stamps. The welfare state provided not only resources to the home, it also literally put a roof over millions of families' heads. Spending on public housing increased from roughly $15 million in 1950 to more than $9 billion by 1985.[23] The racial demographics of the program were striking. Despite being only 12 percent of the population in 1985, 42 percent of AFDC families were black.[24] This was hardly a surprise given that the poverty rate for black female-headed families with children under eighteen was 59 percent.[25]

Family structure was a key element of welfare policy, given that married couples, regardless of need, were ineligible for AFDC in some states.[26] States had discretion to set eligibility rules, and several also deemed families ineligible for the program if an able-bodied man (e.g. boyfriend), considered a "substitute father," regularly had sexual relations with an AFDC mother in her home.[27] The Supreme Court struck down this "man-in-the-house" rule in the 1968 *King v. Smith* case. The unanimous decision rejected the idea that an unrelated male in the home was truly a "substitute father."[28] Politicians and bureaucrats, however, had no problem playing that role. The expansion of welfare programs, particularly AFDC, made the federal government the de facto husband for millions of poor women across the country.

The "Super-Sexist" Marriage

Like every courtship, Uncle Sam's "proposal" to poor black women could not lead to a permanent union without their acceptance. Many single mothers were willing to say "I do" because the feminization of anti-poverty efforts made welfare a major battlefront in the women's liberation movement. Their implicit yes does not, however, mean they were fulfilled in their new relationships.

Johnnie Tillmon was a welfare rights activist who worked to increase the number of black women accessing aid programs. She became a leader within the National Welfare Rights Organization (NWRO) in the 1960s and was its president when it disbanded in the 1970s. Tillmon wrote an essay in *Ms.* magazine that was both perceptive and prescient.

> Welfare is like a super-sexist marriage. You trade in a man for the man. But you can't divorce him if he treats you bad.[29]

Johnnie Tillmon stated that 99 percent of welfare families at the time were headed by women, but despite the state's controlling nature, she still saw government aid as a way to "liberate" poor women.[30] She desired more from the government—*the man*—even as she resented the authority this new patriarch exerted over poor single mothers like herself.

In ordinary marriage, sex is supposed to be for your husband. On AFDC, you're not supposed to have any sex at all. You give up control of your own body. It's a condition of aid. You may even have to agree to get your tubes tied so you can never have more children just to avoid being cut off welfare.

The man, the welfare system, controls your money. He tells you what to buy, what not to buy, where to buy it, and how much things cost. If things—rent, for instance—really cost more than he says they do, it's just too bad for you. He's always right.[31]

Though Johnnie Tillmon was fighting to *increase* the number of black women on welfare, she acknowledged the ways in which the system stripped women of their agency and dignity. Her work gave the illusion of promoting female empowerment, but the women who accepted Uncle Sam's proposal were mired in cultural quicksand—demanding more support while sinking deeper into dependency.

A 2019 NPR profile of the welfare rights movement noted that Tillmon and the other black women on the front lines practiced a style of activism that "centered on autonomy and determination for poor black mothers."[32] That characterization makes sense in the world of big government paternalism, but there is nothing autonomous about a woman who seeks independence from *her* man while becoming dependent on—in Tillmon's words—*the man.*

The paternalism of the welfare state contributed to the destruction of the traditional family structure that was the norm in black America by assuming the roles and responsibilities that historically belonged to men. The harsh realities of slavery created incentives for black men and women to keep their families together. Welfare, by contrast, created powerful incentives for a woman *not* to marry the father of her children. It also gave a father who abandoned his children the knowledge that other men—in this case politicians and bureaucrats—would take care of them. Over time, men began to drift further from their families, a cultural shift that destabilized individual households and entire communities in subsequent decades.

Uncle Sam's Offspring

In a 1992 campaign ad, then-presidential candidate Bill Clinton pledged to "end welfare as we know it" and break the cycle of government dependency.[33] The president made good on his promise when he signed the Personal Responsibility and Work Opportunity Reconciliation Act into law in 1996. It was a very controversial piece of legislation, despite receiving bipartisan support. The feminist push to see poverty as a woman's issue was successful, which meant that changes to the welfare state—including replacing AFDC with the TANF program—were framed as attacks on poor mothers and their children. The new law ended welfare as an entitlement program, placed a five-year limit on benefits paid by the federal government, and included work requirements for individuals receiving benefits. The purpose of the law and restructured programs was to promote responsibility instead of incentivizing dependency. It certainly was successful at reducing the number of families relying on government aid, but no amount of reform could reverse the destructive effect welfare expansion had on the black family since the 1960s.

American families of every background look drastically different today than they did decades ago, but as the saying goes, "when

America catches a cold, black America gets pneumonia." Nothing makes that statement clearer than the state of the black family today, especially because broken homes became the norm in black America *after* the passage of civil rights laws that outlawed racial discrimination and protected voting rights.

Black families were largely intact one generation before the rise of big government paternalism in the era of Jim Crow, even as the non-marital birth rate increased from 16.8 percent in 1940 to 21.6 percent in 1960.[34] Changes in family structure came much more quickly one generation after the expansion of welfare, with out-of-wedlock births among black women rising from 37.6 percent in 1970 to 66.5 percent in 1990.[35]

Seven in ten black children have been born to unmarried parents since the middle of the 1990s.[36] Let's put that in context: More than 70 percent of black children were born to married parents in 1965—a century after the abolition of slavery. Today, only 30 percent are.[37] This may seem counterintuitive to most people, but the facts are clear: The black family was more intact after three centuries of chattel slavery than after three generations of the federal government's "war" on poverty.

One of the cultural transformations social scientists have been following for more than a decade is how marriage morphed from an institution common across socioeconomic class to a "luxury good" found mainly among the educated and upwardly mobile.[38] The marriage-before-carriage model that was the norm in working-class black communities in previous generations is increasingly rare today. In many of these neighborhoods, the government continues to provide cash assistance and pay for food, shelter, health care, and child-care for unmarried mothers and their children.

Things look far more promising on the surface for educated, middle-class black professionals. As is often the case, however, life is not always what it seems. One analysis of birth data found that the nonmarital birth rate increased from 23 percent in 1990 to 33 percent in 2016 among black women with at least a bachelor's degree.[39] This means that out-of-wedlock births are higher among the most educated black women today than they were for *all* black women when the Moynihan Report was published. They are also higher among some of the richest black men in America. The May 4, 1998, issue of *Sports Illustrated* put a little black boy on its cover to ask a question on behalf of children all across the country: "Where's Daddy?" With just one photo and two words, the publication used professional sports to address an issue that had vexed policymakers for decades: the rise in children being born out of wedlock. While *SI* took note of a handful of white players facing paternity suits, including Larry Bird, most of the athletes featured in its special report were black.[40]

The story began with Larry Johnson, an NBA All-Star, traveling to a genetics clinic in California for a paternity test. The blood test Johnson took established paternity, confirming him as the father of five children by four women, including two with his wife of three years.[41] Fellow NBA star Shawn Kemp's seven children made Johnson's tribe look small in comparison. The paternity suit filed against him was initiated by the mother of his two-year-old daughter, who claimed that Kemp told her he had children with five other women. The stories in *SI*'s report were a microcosm of broader societal trends, considering that roughly 70 percent of black children at the time were born to unmarried parents.[42] One sociology professor quoted in the report gave an explanation that fit the men he was discussing like a jersey two sizes too small.

> Class and socioeconomics play the big roles. In middle-class situations people engage in sex just as much, but there's a

different sense of future. I think if people in the underclass felt like their future would be derailed by the pregnancy, they would be more circumspect.[43]

Financial hardship might be a persuasive explanation for broken families in the poorest parts of the cities where these athletes played. Their issue, however, was not a lack of money. Millionaire athletes have the means to care for a family. Some might have feared losing all they worked for in a divorce, but paying child support for multiple children until each one turns eighteen is also a costly endeavor.

All of the children in *SI's* report are adults now. Many probably have families of their own. Unfortunately, several high-profile athletes have followed in the footsteps of the players who preceded them. In 2009, former running back Travis Henry had at least eleven children by ten women.[44] As of 2017, retired cornerback Antonio Cromartie had fourteen children by eight women.[45] Cam Newton, a former NFL quarterback who won an MVP award and played in the Super Bowl, claims eight children, as of 2024, with three women.[46] While the sheer number of children all three men fathered is an outlier, the disconnection of marriage and "carriage" had become the norm in many neighborhoods long before it became fodder for the country's most popular sports magazine.

These changes to black marriage patterns and family life are staggering. They were aided and abetted by public policy, but federal law and local programs are no longer the main reason that "carriage" preceding marriage remains the norm and not the exception. Since the 1960s, black men and women—like all Americans—have been getting married less and later in life. The destabilizing effect of the government's attempts to help the black family are seen and felt far more in the urban core than anywhere else. Today, there are entire neighborhoods where it is rare for a black child to be raised his entire childhood in a home with his married father and mother. Policy cannot solve this issue, but it certainly helped cause it.

Conclusion

One of the most common assumptions about the black family and welfare is that the "man-in-the-house" rule pushed black men out of their homes. History tells a different story. The changes made to AFDC in the 1960s made it possible for multiple generations of women to raise children without a man in the home. It's not that men were forcefully pushed out, but rather that AFDC allowed a man to abdicate the financial responsibility he had for his family and encouraged the mother of his children to look to the government for protection and provision. The most lasting impact of the government playing the role of "substitute father" is not the size of welfare rolls or the growth of the federal bureaucracy. It is the destabilizing effect on how men and women form families. The Moynihan Report spoke about welfare dependency as a symptom of divorce, separation, and "illegitimacy" among poor urban blacks. In the decades that followed, these programs became a major *cause* of the family breakdown he warned about in 1965. While big-government paternalism helped set this pattern of broken families in place, the culture that developed over generations in response to policy incentives in welfare programs did not magically disappear when reforms were enacted in the 1990s.

The principle of sowing and reaping is as true in the creation of family culture as it is in agriculture. In both instances, what you plant and nourish not only grows but also reproduces itself. The more families break apart and men fail to fulfill their God-given roles, the more government aid is needed to sustain the low-income women raising children. When this change grows from a handful of families to entire neighborhoods, it sends two important signals. The first is that marrying before having children is not necessary, whether socially or economically. The second is that men are not needed in the home as husbands and fathers as long as there are government programs that will take care of needy families. Both lessons continue the cycle of fractured families, an important reminder that, as the Moynihan Report noted, culture is often self-perpetuating and capable of survival even when the factors that contributed to its development have subsided.

Decades of paternalism have done serious structural damage to the foundation of the black family. Even President Johnson's Howard University speech previewing his Great Society programs was built on a shaky foundation, in part because one of his most famous quotes cast African Americans as supporting actors in their own autobiographies. The US government didn't "bring" emancipated blacks up to the starting line. The people who endured slavery started to run their race as soon as the shackles of bondage were removed. They rebuilt their families, educated themselves, created institutions, built businesses, and started free communities. Progress was not universal and did not close all the "gaps" that frustrate policymakers, but the most important structures—family and faith—were solid. The cracks that started to appear in the black family deserved attention, but the president's mistake was thinking he and his administration had the power to fix them by giving more money to single mothers.

Progressives today have the same problem. They reject the idea that family structure has any bearing on social outcomes and make their promotion of the welfare state all about lifting single mothers and their children out of poverty. This has been the reality facing the black family for more than sixty years. It has been studied, analyzed, dissected, and discussed by people who present themselves as friends and allies. But neither condescension nor neglect will repair the black family. Outsourcing agency to external parties will not do it either. The only way things change is if the people affected by the problem take ownership of it, exercise responsibility for solving it, and invite friends and allies—when appropriate—to *help* them along the way.

The black family survived chattel slavery and endured every storm that battered the home in the century between the end of the Civil War and the end of the civil rights movement. It survived every direct attack from its enemies, but the people who came as "friends" offering "help" undermined the structure that makes families strong. They turned the government into a substitute father while claiming to fight for families. Liberal paternalists displaced black patriarchs, altering the role of men in both their homes and communities for decades to come.

The destruction of the traditional black family, however, was not a one-sided affair. While big government liberals thought their policies would "help" black families, second-wave feminists in the 1960s targeted women with hostility to the institution of marriage and the social norms that governed family formation at the time. Anyone interested in the truth about the current state of the black family must understand the ideological revolution that deceived black women into seeing black men as oppressors, the home as a prison, and their children as a burden.

THREE

Deceive Women
with Feminism

Eboni K. Williams is a lawyer, television host, and the first black cast member on *The Real Housewives of New York City*. The veteran media personality is everything modern women want to be: attractive, educated, accomplished, and influential. To the outside world, she has it all. But a few years ago, Williams went public with the one thing she desperately desired but had not attained: a family. Rather than sitting around waiting for her Prince Charming, Williams began publicly promoting the idea of becoming a single mother—by choice. She unpacked her plan while hosting a news program on TheGrio by stating that "single motherhood by choice is going to be an option that more and more black women consider," later noting that these women "will increasingly decide to forego marriages and partnerships that do not serve" them.

Williams showed no hesitation when challenging the traditional marriage-before-carriage life script that is still the norm for the upper middle class today. What was striking, however, was how she talked about fulfilling her desire to be a mother. She claimed that most black women on this "journey" want babies who look like them and their families, which means that these single mothers by choice need, in her words, "black sperm."

Williams used that phrase six times in her pitch to other black women and even advised them to stockpile the reproductive material and give away their unused supply to friends.[1] No one was surprised when Williams was pregnant a year later and discussing why she was "proud" to be a single mom by choice in a glowing profile by *People* magazine.[2] Williams, who was raised by a single mother, said that in just one generation, the stigma associated with being a black mother with no husband had faded. She didn't see her choice as solely an exercise in self-fulfillment. She also believed it was good for children, noting that women like her invested "exorbitant resources" to "shower them with all the things that all sweet babies deserve. That's love."[3] Williams may be rich, but there is one thing her money can't buy: the love from a father that every child—including hers—needs. But the message Williams wanted to send to her peers was loud and clear: The traditional family is obsolete, and an economically independent black woman doesn't need a husband to have a baby.

A 2022 *Washington Post* article about the shortage of black male sperm donors and the women competing for the short supply sent the same message.[4] One woman in the article expressed her desire for an African American donor but, along with her girlfriend at the time, turned her attention to Latino donors when her cryobank returned only three black men out of more than a hundred after she filtered for her racial preference. She was newly single by the time she gave birth to a daughter that she conceived with sperm from a Peruvian donor, but she still believed there were "so many good African American men out there," adding that many "just don't know how much they're needed to create families."[5] The ease with which black men were written out of her idea of a "family" should raise alarm bells, but she is far from the only person in our society who has learned to value men for their resources—in this case their reproductive capacity—and little else.

Another woman, described as a "single lesbian," subscribed to a donor app called Just a Baby and was matched with a married father of four near her home.[6] What follows next is an example of family dysfunction on full display.

> A couple of months later, the two met at a restaurant, went to a hotel and used a DIY at-home insemination kit. After the first attempt didn't work, they used the insemination kit and had sex the next month to increase the chance of pregnancy.[7]

Perhaps the man's wife supported his desires to have sex with other women and father children outside of their marriage. If not, his infidelity adds only more chaos and confusion to a story about intentional fatherlessness that will impact two different families, perhaps over multiple generations. The women who want babies but not husbands are unconcerned about how the absence of a father harms a child. The women in this story also saw men as a means to create the families of their dreams, not partners needed to raise a baby. One of the women profiled who chose to pursue single motherhood said she believes "there is a true and divine right of women to create the lives of their choosing."[8]

Williams's story reflects the new reality of modern family life, but the seeds of her decision to become a single mother by choice were planted long before she went on the hunt for "black sperm." The absurd cultural attitude toward sex, gender roles, and family that fuels her story are a direct result of the second-wave feminist movement that began in the 1960s—and the glowing coverage of a movement for families without fathers shows how successful feminists were at achieving their goals.

Indeed, feminists began writing men out of the family script long ago. In the 1960s, the movement's leaders aimed to change social norms and were vocal about their dissatisfaction with the breadwinner husband/homemaking wife approach to family life. Feminists promised women "liberation" and deceived them into thinking that wives were oppressed by their husbands, imprisoned by their homes, and burdened by their children. By their logic, women could achieve true freedom only when at least two conditions were met. The first was a cultural environment that said women don't need marriage or family to be happy and fulfilled. The second was a path to education and financial independence so that they would not need to rely on men to achieve economic security or to start families.

The marriage-optional approach to family formation is now the norm in black America: Today, less than 30 percent of black households comprise married couples, a rate far lower than for any other group. How did we get here? In order for the feminist movement to influence the family, they first needed to rebrand the home as a prison.

Prison Break

Betty Friedan's 1963 book *The Feminine Mystique* is widely credited with sparking the second-wave feminist movement. Friedan coined the term "feminine mystique" to describe the idea that women found fulfillment playing the roles of wife and mother and had no interest in matters outside the home.[9] The author, activist, and cofounder of the National Organization for Women believed that the suburban housewife, largely focused on her family and domestic life, was trapped in a "comfortable concentration camp" where she was destined to a "slow death of mind and spirit."[10]

Liberal feminists like Friedan wanted to work within existing social structures to give women more autonomy—over both their finances and their bodies. Gloria Steinem wrote a *Time* magazine essay in 1970 entitled "What Would It Be Like If Women Win" that began with the claim that women "don't want to exchange places with men" and continued on to describe a "Women's Lib Utopia" where women are equally represented in every aspect of society.[11] Not only did Steinem envision women in politics and the corporate world, she also believed men would benefit from not having to shoulder the burden of providing for a family.[12] Steinem hoped for revised sex roles and did not believe they would have a significant impact on the relationship between men and women. In fact, she explicitly stated, "Women's Lib is not trying to destroy the American family."[13]

Whether the overt goal was to upend the family or merely provide women more economic opportunity, mainstream liberal feminists of the 1960s all challenged the social norms and gender dynamics that kept women at home playing the role of, in Steinem's words, "housekeeper" and "hostess."[14] The *Black Women's Manifesto*, a highly influential document in the development of black feminist thought published in 1970 by the Third World Women's Alliance, used similar rhetoric in its hostility toward women in the home.

> There is no reason to repeat bad history. There is no reason to envy the white woman who is sinking in a sea of close-quartered affluence, where one's world is one's house, one's peers one's children, and one's employer one's husband.[15]

Black Feminists, White Masters

It is important to note that second-wave black feminists represented a stark departure from—and actively undermined—previous generations of educated black women who had very different views on the role they played in the struggle for racial uplift.

Anna Julia Cooper was a prominent scholar, educator, and activist who is considered the "mother of black feminism."[16] She was a champion of liberal arts education for black students, including girls, who were barely one generation removed from slavery. But the views she expressed on the importance of the home in her 1892 book, *A Voice from the South*, sound much different from those of the second-wave black feminists who came after her. From her work:

> The earnest well trained Christian young woman, as a teacher, as a home-maker, as wife, mother, or silent influence even, is as potent a missionary agency among our people as is the theologian; and I claim that at the present stage of our development in the South she is even more important and necessary.[17]

Cooper was not alone in her assessment. Rosetta Douglass Sprague, the eldest child of Frederick Douglass and his first wife Anna, wrote that the "educated Negro woman will find that her greatest field for effective work is in the home."[18] Mary Church Terrell, a founding member of the National Association of Colored Women, wrote that "it is through the home that a people can become really good and truly great" before declaring her organization's intent to enter that "sacred domain" to teach black women not far removed from slavery how to manage their households and raise children.[19] Terrell, like Cooper, saw the home as the primary training ground for cultivating virtue in children, which explains why their writings frequently reference industry, honesty, temperance, and godliness.

The concern black women had for the state of the family continued throughout the twentieth century. Dorothy Height, president of the National Council of Negro Women, understood that the fortunes of black men were directly connected to the well-being of their families. Her comments in 1963 would likely have been seen as traitorous by black feminists of the 1970s.

> If the Negro woman has a major underlying concern, it is the status of the Negro man and his position in the community and his need for feeling himself an important person, free and able to make his contribution in the whole society in order that he may strengthen his home.[20]

None of the educators and activists fighting for the rights of black women prior to 1965 were arguing women should be concerned only about their homes. These women started organizations for the uplift of the race, local clubs to meet the needs of their neighbors, labor organizations to help women gain marketable skills, and schools to educate the next generation of children. Nannie Helen Burroughs' National Training School for Women and Girls was often called the "The School of the 3 Bs." This was a reference to the Bible, bath, and broom and reflected her emphasis on Christian morality, cleanliness, and home maintenance.[21]

Black women like Cooper, Terrell, and Height were also active in fighting against Jim Crow laws, lynchings, and other political and cultural realities that prevented black Americans from enjoying the full benefits of citizenship. They made extensive contributions to the upward trajectory of the race in the century after emancipation. That means black scholars and activists in the early stages of the second-wave feminist movement had role models to show them how an education could be used for the good of individual women, their families, and the race.

In a cruel twist of irony, the next wave of black feminists committed themselves to tearing down the family instead of building it up. Their scholarship and activism injected strife and discord into the relationships between black men and women. They often mocked African American women who they believed romanticized the roles of housewife and mother, attributing their views to societal conditioning based on white, middle-class norms.[22] They wanted black women to reject traditional gender roles and family life in order to commit themselves to "throwing off the yoke of capitalist oppression."[23] The black feminists writing at the time wanted to see women pursuing higher education and filling the roles in society and the economy they believed were needed to wage a revolution. In their words, black women "sitting at home reading bedtime stories to their children are just not going to make it."[24]

Despite expressing similar views on the oppression of women—and sometimes offering similar prescriptions to fix the problems they saw—black scholars in the 1970s nonetheless believed that the mainstream feminist movement reflected the interests of middle-class white women. The *Combahee River Collective Statement*, published in 1977, is one of the most important texts in black feminism, in part because it describes capitalism, racism, and sexism as "interlocking" systems of oppression. The authors believed their fight for freedom required embracing "identity politics" that focused explicitly on the needs of black women. One important way early black feminists differed from their white peers was that they saw black men as potential allies in their struggle for liberation.

> Although we are feminists and lesbians, we feel solidarity with progressive Black men and do not advocate the fractionalization that white women who are separatists demand. Our situation as Black people necessitates that we have solidarity around the fact of race, which white women of course do not need to have with white men, unless it is their negative solidarity as racial oppressors. We struggle together with Black men against racism, while we also struggle with Black men about sexism.[25]

It is no surprise that the women of the Combahee River Collective and many other notable black feminists were lesbians. Others remained unmarried for life or had white spouses. Their views on black men, combined with a commitment to upending social norms, demonstrate the intersection of the personal and political. Second-wave black feminists followed the lead of their white mainstream contemporaries instead of the example set by their intellectual foremothers. Audre Lorde is famous for saying the "master's tools will never dismantle the master's house," but given how black feminists wrote about black men and the traditional family, it's clear they used the tools of their white masters to destroy their own.

This struggle between the sexes has been a consistent theme in black feminist scholarship since it emerged as a distinct political philosophy. Writers would declare their love for black men as comrades in the battle against racism in one sentence and critique their embrace of patriarchal thinking in the next. At times, they were critical of the abuse and infidelity that women in previous generations endured, but their issues with masculinity ran far deeper. Patricia

Hill Collins's book *Black Feminist Thought* cites a scholar who argues "protecting black women was the most significant measure of black manhood and the central aspect of black male patriarchy."[26] Black men defending black women seems uncontroversial. But the analysis of this dynamic that followed displays the adversarial lens through which black feminists viewed the relationship between the sexes.

> If Omolade is correct, then this important choice to protect Black women, for many men, became harnessed to ideologies of Black masculinity in such a way that Black manhood became dependent on Black women's willingness to accept protection. Within this version of masculinity, a slippery slope emerges between *protecting* Black women and *controlling* them.[27]

This is one of the clearest examples of the complex—and contradictory—nature of black feminism. Writers would lament black men's inability to protect black women during slavery, then claim that later generations of men who prioritized their role as guardians of the home were being driven by sexist impulses. Similarly, they wrote about the oppression of working as domestic servants for white people—cleaning their homes and caring for their children—before accusing black women who stayed at home caring for their *own* children of a "parasitic existence that can aptly be described as "legalized prostitution."[28] This way of thinking reveals an important reality: The anti-family nature of feminism is an ideological feature, not a bug. A political ideology marked by hostility between the sexes can't produce healthy marriages and strong families. In fact, it can lead only to conflict and division in the home. To quote Proverbs 14:1, "The wise woman builds her house, but with her own hands the foolish one tears hers down."

At their core, black feminists writing in the 1970s saw themselves as revolutionaries preparing to wage war against white supremacy, capitalism, and the patriarchy. When they weren't attacking their male counterparts, they saw them merely as useful tools for achieving a utopian end, not as husbands with whom they could build families. This social dynamic still exists within black feminism today. Brittney Cooper, a self-described radical feminist, wrote in a 2015 *Salon* column that "we should celebrate the fact that the two-parent, nuclear family ideal has gone the way of the floppy disk."[29] She has made similar claims on social media over the years. In fact, I challenged her pro-family bona fides after seeing a video of her claiming, "we want to build strong, healthy black families." She responded to my rebuke with a now-deleted tweet:

> We don't need traditional nuclear families for Black thriving. As one raised by my mother, grandmother and aunts I can attest. We should support families however they are configured to provide basic needs in loving and safe environments. That's what being pro-Black family means.[30]

Cooper's perspective might sound radical to some, but it's easy to see why she would believe fathers are optional. Early black feminists preached the gospel of self-empowerment, independence, and revolution. Their evangelistic efforts proved quite fruitful, as a growing number of women have come to rethink the roles marriage and family play in their pursuit of happiness. Black feminists eventually resolved the gender struggle they have had with black men by finding new partners who promised freedom from the men oppressing them and the children weighing them down.

Love Triangle

As the previous chapter highlighted, the expansion of the welfare state placed elected officials and unelected bureaucrats in the role of husband and father for millions of single mothers and their children. Groups such as the National Welfare Rights Organization convinced many poor black women that Uncle Sam would be a better—and less oppressive—partner to them than the black men who fathered their children.[31]

Feminism's war on the family was enabled through policy decisions that increased government support to single mothers in the 1960s. But the incorporation of feminist ideology into the modern progressive movement has turned discussions about marriage and family structure from a policy issue to a partisan political issue. The dissolution of the black family since the mid-1960s has been aided and incentivized by the symbiotic relationship between single mothers, government administrators, and liberal politicians.

Progressive candidates promise more government spending on social welfare programs, largely for unmarried mothers, that are administered by bureaucrats. Everyone in this scenario has something to gain. Politicians gain power, professionals in the poverty economy get job security, and low-income women receive financial support. In this arrangement, black men play a role in procreation but not in household leadership. For black feminists, this is the perfect relationship. Uncle Sam provides food and shelter for poor single mothers and supports the career aspirations of educated and upwardly mobile black women. The fact that a growing number of government leaders, whether elected or appointed, are black women makes the union that much stronger.

There were five black members of Congress when the Civil Rights Act of 1964 became law.[32] There were more than sixty serving in the 118th Congress sixty years later.[33] More than 40 percent of black congressional representatives are women.[34] Likewise, some of the largest cities in America, including Los Angeles, Chicago, Atlanta, Washington, DC, Baltimore, St. Louis, New Orleans, have all had black female mayors. And of course there was Kamala Harris, who ran for president after serving four years as Joe Biden's vice president. Biden's selection of Harris, combined with his pledge to appoint the first black woman to the Supreme Court, shows how Democrats moved their support of black women beyond social programs for poor mothers to political patronage for their most loyal supporters. The irony is that as a nominee Justice Ketanji Brown Jackson refused to define the word "woman," but that didn't stop her appointment from being hailed as a milestone by black feminists.

Black women in public office represent the intersectional triumph of black feminist politics—if they are loyal to progressive causes. Like most liberals, they support more government programs such as social welfare benefits for single mothers and their children, job training, free childcare, and housing vouchers. They differ from the white liberals in previous decades because they also embody the rejection of black male leadership that was the default in the civil rights era. At times this paradigm shift takes the form of open hostility toward black men. Sunny Hostin, co-host of *The View*, called black men voting for Donald Trump in 2024 "ridiculous" and "crazy" without any pushback from her colleagues.[35] That sentiment was expressed by other black women in politics and media in each of Trump's campaigns. Some women are better at hiding their dismissive attitudes under a facade of concern. In 2022, former MSNBC host Tiffany Cross told black men in Georgia to "get in line" behind black women and vote for Stacey Abrams for governor.[36] Cross spoke to the men in her audience as if they had no agency because she knows that when it comes to black political power, women like herself and Abrams run the show.

At other times, the progressive posture toward black men is marked by neglect. Democrats frequently refer to black women as the "backbone" of their party and "saviors" of democracy. Their messaging to black men, however, sounds much different. How? Look at the black men liberals elevate. The reason progressive politicians talk so much about George Floyd, Jacob Blake, and Michael Brown is because black men play the role of noble victims in their cultural imagination. The subtext of liberal messaging to black men is "vote for us and we will keep you from being killed by the police." Black voters show up in large numbers at the polls, and the party responds by promising black *women* positions of power and leadership.

Black feminists have powerful incentives to maintain the status quo because they benefit from the "political patriarchy" within the interracial marriage they have had with white liberals for decades. This relationship has helped black women amass political power and cultural influence, an arrangement that has exacerbated existing gender conflicts. Black men on the left—pushed out of this political marriage—know they must demonstrate fealty to progressive gender and sexual politics to stay in the good graces of black women. They have learned over the years that playing the role of dutiful feminist ally is the best way to shield themselves from spurious accusations of sexism. This explains why Roland Martin, a prominent media figure with a large black audience, posted a picture of himself on social media wearing a shirt that had "Vote Like a Black Woman" written across his chest.[37] Men like him know that appeasing black women is a good strategy for survival within the left's political ecosystem. They also understand that the support is not reciprocal. Martin may tell black men in his audience to follow their wives to the polls, but none of his female counterparts in media would wear a shirt saying "Lead Like a Black Man."

This complex interaction between race, gender, and politics explains why Democrats rarely discuss marriage and family structure today. A party that fully embraces feminism, financially supports single mothers, and openly upholds black women as leaders in their homes and communities has no incentive to promote traditional family values. This is seen most clearly in the left's views on children.

Baby Burdens

No single issue drives home the deceptive and self-destructive nature of feminism more than abortion. While men play a necessary role in reproduction, the fact remains that every single human being on the planet was birthed by a woman. Feminists look at occupations and activities reserved for men as potential battlegrounds for gender equality but treat women's exclusive capacity to bring forth life like a disease to be cured, not a sacred responsibility to be cherished. While demographers and policymakers look at fertility rates to predict whether there will be enough workers to maintain social programs, the true beauty of motherhood is felt when a woman embraces her child for the first time and when the baby she has been carrying for nine months seeks the same attachment and connection outside the womb as she did in utero.

A new baby has traditionally been viewed as a blessing by the child's parents, grandparents, extended family, and community. Second-wave feminists, however, encouraged women to reject—and at times despise—the role they play in the human life cycle. To them, destroying your offspring is one of the most important ways to "smash the patriarchy," especially when a baby would interfere with a woman's educational pursuits or career goals.

The desire to give women control over when, and under what circumstances, they give birth goes back further than the *Roe v. Wade* Supreme Court decision in 1973. Margaret Sanger, founder of Planned Parenthood, opened her first birth control clinic in Brooklyn in 1916.[38] The Food and Drug Administration approved the first oral contraceptive pill in 1960.[39] The widespread use of contraception coincided with both the second-wave feminist movement and the sexual revolution. Men who wanted to have as much sex with as many people as they desired could always walk away from an unplanned pregnancy. Feminists argued that birth control and abortion allowed women to do the same. They believed securing women the legal right to terminate a pregnancy advanced the cause of liberation, especially for the women who wanted to pursue their dreams without the responsibility of having children. Feminist scholar bell hooks expressed the baby burden phenomenon in her book *Feminism Is for Everybody*.

> Many of us were the unplanned children of talented, creative women whose lives had been changed by unplanned and unwanted pregnancies; we witnessed their bitterness, their rage, their disappointment with their lot in life. And we were clear that there could be no genuine sexual liberation for women and men without better, safer contraceptives—without the right to a safe, legal abortion.[40]

Abortion epitomizes the destructive effect feminism has had on the African American family in that it is framed as the apex of both female empowerment and black liberation. Somehow, for all their talk of fighting racism, the black feminist position on abortion advances the same position on the black population—the fewer, the better—you would expect to hear from a Klansman in the 1940s. This sentiment has been a prominent part of the public discourse in the wake of the 2022 *Dobbs v. Jackson* Supreme Court decision that struck down *Roe*. *Vox*, a popular progressive news site, published the headline "Black Women Will Suffer the Most Without Roe."[41] One opinion piece in *Politico* made the connection between feminists, race politics, and abortion crystal clear with the headline "I'm Black. I Thought White Feminism Would Keep Abortion Safe."[42]

Though promoting the elimination of black children is, on its face, neither pro-black nor pro-woman, none of these headlines should come as a surprise. Progressive politics is one of the main reasons abortion is now seen as a key battlefront in the fight for both gender and racial justice. In 2016, black women in New York City had 22,123 live births and 21,990 induced abortions.[43] That year was no anomaly. Close to half of all black women's pregnancies in America's largest city end in abortion, yet these disparities provoke little public debate among activists who champion the value of black life.[44] The racial disparities in the South are just as striking. African Americans make up 38 percent of Mississippi's population, 33 percent of Georgia's, and 27 percent of Alabama's. Yet, according to the Centers for Disease Control (CDC), in 2021 80 percent of the babies aborted in Mississippi were black, along with 69 percent in Georgia and 64 percent in Alabama.[45] Anyone familiar with antiracist activists knows they blame racism for all social and economic disparities between blacks and whites. Progressives are equally vocal about threats to the "black body" when they bring up police shootings and incarceration rates. For some reason they make an exception for abortion. The political left understands it can promote abortion, despite glaring racial disparities, if pro-life laws are framed as attempts to control women's bodies and "white supremacy."

Another important disparity highlighted in the CDC's report was the connection between abortion and marital status. Close to 90 percent of women seeking abortions are unmarried.[46] This suggests that the breakdown of the black family is fueling the abortion industry that destroys a disproportionate number of black babies every year. Unfortunately, influential civil rights organizations are far more passionate about preserving abortion than rebuilding the black family. The NAACP, National Urban League, and National Action Network joined with Planned Parenthood in the wake of *Dobbs* to demand a meeting with the White House to discuss the "disproportionate impact" the decision would have on black women. The nation's largest abortion provider has its hooks in far more than legacy civil rights outfits. The Congressional Black Caucus, BET, and some of the most popular black entertainers all draw a connection between women's empowerment and abortion, seemingly ignorant of the irony alongside their public proclamations that "black lives matter."

Despite the sacrosanctity of abortion to feminists in decades past, as well as Democrats today, acceptance among black leaders has never been universal. Fannie Lou Hamer was a civil rights activist who fought to register black voters in the Jim Crow South. She was also staunchly pro-life, claiming abortion was "legal murder" that amounted to "genocide."[47] Mildred Jefferson was the first black woman to graduate from Harvard Medical School in 1951 and was active in the pro-life movement throughout her life.[48] Even Rev. Jesse Jackson was a vocal defender of the unborn in the immediate aftermath of *Roe*. In the March 22, 1973, edition of *Jet* magazine, the civil rights leader stated his position plainly: "Abortion is genocide."[49] The same story quoted the Black Panther Party on its anti-abortion stance: "The abortion law hides behind the guise of helping women when in reality it will attempt to destroy our people."[50] That position did not last long. Elaine Brown became the first female leader of the Black Panther Party in 1974 and shifted the organization's stance on the issue significantly, claiming:

> I would support every assertion of human rights by women—
> from the right to abortion to the right of equality with men
> as laborers and leaders.[51]

No organization that actually cares about black people would support killing unborn black babies, regardless of how much it cloaked its death agenda in the language of "revolution" and "liberation." Thankfully, there are black advocates, activists, and politicians today who aren't swayed by pro-abortion arguments framed in racial justice terms. Men like Tony Dungy and Benjamin Watson made careers in the NFL and today are among the most prominent pro-life voices in the country. Likewise, despite the party's embrace of abortion without restrictions, state legislators like Katrina Jackson in Louisiana and Treneé McGee in Connecticut prove that pro-life Democrats are not completely extinct. But these lonely voices are exceptional in the truest sense of the word, given how committed most Democrats are to promoting abortion as a net positive for the black community.

Conclusion

While Betty Friedan and Gloria Steinem are revered as leaders in the second-wave feminist movement, the insufficient attention paid to race by the white mainstream was a major blind spot that created intellectual space for a more intersectional version of feminism to develop. Alice Walker, author of *The Color Purple*, eventually coined the term "womanism" to focus on the concerns of black women and the unique challenges they face in a world hostile to both their race and sex. This explains why the work of black feminists like Walker, bell hooks, Angela Davis, and Audre Lorde has been far more influential on political discourse and activism in the black community than that of their white peers.

Their work kicked off more than half a century of black feminist hostility toward men, marriage, and family. Alice Walker's daughter, Rebecca, shared her experience with becoming a mother in 2008 and noted that being raised by a "rabid feminist" almost made her miss out on having a child.[52] Rebecca, a noted feminist author in her own right, perfectly captured the hostility her mother Alice and her contemporaries had toward the family.

> It was drummed into me that being a mother, raising children and running a home were a form of slavery. Having a career, travelling the world and being independent were what really mattered according to her.[53]

The daughter rejected the views of her iconic mother and said having a child was the most rewarding experience of her life.[54] She stated, "feminism has much to answer for denigrating men and encouraging women to seek independence whatever the cost to their families," before noting that her mother had never seen her only grandchild.[55]

The independence movement promoted by feminists since the 1960s has largely been successful. Black women today earn about

65 percent of bachelor's degrees and roughly 70 percent of Master's degrees and PhDs awarded to African Americans.[56] Median weekly earnings for black women are $942, compared with $1,053 for black men—the smallest gap among the major ethnic groups.[57] Further, among black homebuyers, single women (27 percent) account for more than twice the purchases as single men (13 percent).[58] Unfortunately, feminists were promoting far more than educational and economic opportunities for women. They also encouraged women to view men as their enemy, the home as a prison, children as a barrier to true fulfillment, and the traditional family as a construct rooted in "white supremacy."[59] Feminists sowed the seeds of family discord, and the black family has reaped its bitter fruit. Today, only 35 percent of black women are married, and 44 percent between thirty-five and forty-four years old have *never* been married. [60] It bears repeating that less than 30 percent of black households are composed of married couples, a rate far lower than any other group.[61]

Those statistics represent feminism's most significant impact over the past sixty years. The leaders of the movement told women to reject the dominant life script that prioritized marriage and family for a set of new norms that are self-focused. While men are told to embrace the responsibilities and duties that come with a family, the consistent message to women today is about their rights and freedoms. They are encouraged to end any relationship that isn't "serving" them at any given moment, a move frequently characterized as a sign of self-love. *Essence* magazine published a story in 2024 entitled "Stop Criticizing Tia Mowry And Women Like Her For Leaving 'Good' Men" about a popular black actress who divorced her husband of fourteen years. The author's perspective on women and marriage sounds like it was pulled from a 1960s feminist manifesto.

A woman leaving a marriage to pursue her happiness might be selfish by the patriarchy's standards, but it's also brave. Women have been indoctrinated to be selfless and self-sacrificing, and it mostly serves the people who benefit from our oppression.[62]

The elevation of self has been a consistent theme in feminist academic discourse for years, but today it is just as prevalent in mainstream media publications. Tia Mowry proves that destroying your marriage and breaking up a happy home is not seen as a problem in progressive circles if the person doing the destruction is a woman. Eboni K. Williams' decision to intentionally become a single mother shows the same goes for women who want babies but not husbands. Perhaps this is what "winning" looks like in the feminist utopia envisioned by Gloria Steinem and Alice Walker, but nothing about failed marriages, fractured homes, and fatherless children is good for the family.

FOUR

Deny There's a Problem

The Tuskegee Study of Untreated Syphilis in the Negro Male is one of the most infamous research experiments in American history. The study was initiated by the US Public Health Service, in collaboration with the Tuskegee Institute, in 1932 with 399 black men in rural Alabama who had syphilis. Those men could have been treated in the 1940s, when penicillin became the universal standard treatment for syphilis, but they were not. Instead, the physicians who had the knowledge and resources to care for these men allowed them to suffer needlessly for the forty years that the study ran. In fact, the goal of the study was never to treat syphilis but to understand what happens when it goes untreated.

Thankfully, since the study ended with a groundswell of national outrage in 1972, several ethical safeguards have been put in place to protect people who participate in biomedical research. Yet the Tuskegee study casts such a large shadow on the American public health system that it is still cited as one of the main reasons African Americans are skeptical of the medical establishment to this day.[1] For instance, many African Americans referenced the

Tuskegee experiment to explain their initial refusal to take the COVID-19 shot.[2]

There is an aspect of the black family's current condition that can be explained by this kind of negligence. Despite an abundance of highly educated black leaders with power and influence who function as "cultural physicians," the pathogens of radical feminism and big government liberalism have been allowed to spread for decades without a concerted effort to treat their effects on the family. While cultural physicians do not need medical training, many of the same principles that apply to doctors with MDs are also relevant to activists with PhDs. Among them are the responsibilities to observe symptoms of social decline, identify the cause, prescribe a treatment that maximizes the chances of improving future outcomes, and give a prognosis for the future.

But there is another duty cultural physicians must fulfill. They have a responsibility to never intentionally hurt their patients. To be clear, a doctor can cause harm in two distinct ways. The first is connected to the treatments they prescribe. This includes giving a person bad medicine, the wrong medicine, or too much medicine. The second, what I'll call the "Tuskegee effect," is when a doctor *withholds* treatment and allows a patient's condition to get progressively worse. While the first tends to lead to medical malpractice lawsuits that garner major media attention, the second often goes unnoticed and unpunished.

Black leaders have a long track record of playing the role of "cultural physician" throughout American history. Whether it was abolitionists like Frederick Douglass or civil rights leaders like Dr. Martin Luther King Jr., they wielded their moral authority to bring attention to important social and political issues. They observed symptoms of cultural distress, diagnosed problems, and prescribed solutions. Sometimes their focus was on external problems like discriminatory laws, but they were just as likely to speak out about internal issues like violent crime in black neighborhoods. Unfortunately, the people most able to marshal the cultural, social, political, and financial resources needed to address the breakdown of the black family have been largely silent in recent decades. Put simply, they have failed to fulfill the duties that come with leadership and influence.

Today's cultural physicians are typically not concerned with the well-being of the black community. Ibram X. Kendi, for example, says it is his job to "diagnose racism" and "provide treatments."[3] In effect, he runs a surgical center that says "Whites Only" because he believes that healing white people is the most important way to help black people. Kendi is not an anomaly. The most educated black cultural physicians today focus exclusively on the patients *they* claim have the most resources and privilege, while leaving the disenfranchised and destitute in the hospital waiting room. What Kendi and his peers never do is publicly address what black people must do for *ourselves*—aside from protesting and voting—to bring about positive change in our communities. The fight to restore marriage to its rightful place in black family life should be at the top of that list.

Rise of the Afristocracy

The cultural physicians who willingly ignore the obvious signs of familial breakdown betray the long history of black leaders who worked to remove barriers to progress, regardless of their source. W. E. B. DuBois was a sociologist who earned a PhD from Harvard in 1895 and helped found the NAACP in 1909. He is well-known for his belief that racial uplift would be led by an elite group of educated blacks. In his view, "The Talented Tenth of the Negro race must be made leaders of thought and missionaries of culture among their people."[4] Given his personal and professional background, his views on the importance of higher education and belief that the "Negro race" would be "saved by its exceptional men" were unsurprising.

His model of black leadership—an "aristocracy of talent and character"—reflected his belief that civilization never occurs from the bottom up but rather from the top down.[5] DuBois believed that the educated elite should guide the masses away from the "contamination and death" of destructive influences "in their own and other races."[6] This is exactly what black leaders did for much of the twentieth century, because they understood virtue was a prerequisite for racial uplift. Charles Henry Turner, a black biologist born in 1867, wrote that real progress for free blacks in the South would require both "Christian morality" and the "ability to do something well that the world desires bad enough to be willing to pay a good price for it."[7] Men like him understood that while laws and social norms circumscribed the opportunities available to blacks at the time, a man or woman with a marketable skill and good character could make the most out of difficult circumstances. This explains why so much of their work focused on personal conduct and technical skills in addition to broader social conditions. Black leaders at that time felt an obligation to use their time, talent, and treasure to help their less fortunate brethren do better and *be* better.

That is no longer the case among the black progressive politicians, pundits, professors, preachers, and performers who masquerade as the modern Talented Tenth. One reason the black family is in its current state is that the African American leadership class

DuBois promoted has morphed from a morally grounded and socially conscious educated elite into a self-serving "Afristocracy" more concerned with disrupting social norms than preserving them.

While *Afristocracy* evokes images of a black elite class as DuBois described it in the early 1900s, I did not invent the term. Ironically enough, I first read it in the early 2000s in professor and political commentator Michael Eric Dyson's book *Is Bill Cosby Right? Or Has the Black Middle Class Lost Its Mind?* Dyson took Cosby to task for the comedian's infamous "Pound Cake Speech" at an NAACP-sponsored gala commemorating the fiftieth anniversary of *Brown v. Board of Education*. Cosby spoke candidly and critically about the state of family life, education, and personal conduct in the black community.[8] He stated that the black poor were failing to do their part in improving their lives with the freedoms that had been gained over the past century.[9] Cosby was operating like black leaders did for generations but was apparently unaware of how his brand of candid criticism had fallen out of favor by that time.

Dyson cast Cosby as the archetype of his definition of the Afristocracy: upper middle-class blacks and black elites who "rain down fire and brimstone" on poor blacks for their "deviance and pathology."[10] He contrasted this group with the "Ghettocracy"—a group that included single mothers on welfare, felons and ex-offenders, the working poor, and even athletes and entertainers whose values have been shaped by growing up in poverty.[11] Dyson believed Cosby and other black elites were too critical of the behaviors and attitudes that are often attributed to the black poor.

Dyson used the term "Afristocracy" to criticize old-school black elites like Bill Cosby, but in reality, the leadership style he was critiquing in the 2000s was already going extinct. The new Afristocrats are intellectuals and influencers like Dyson who use their advanced education, extensive vocabulary, media platforms, and cultural influence to *excuse* unproductive and self-destructive behaviors in the black community. These black elites reject the belief that racial uplift requires a solid moral foundation and value system. They defend and justify dysfunction instead of correcting it.

Today's Afristocrats reserve their moral indignation and cultural police powers for white people, with occasional rebukes directed at other groups who transgress their racial sensitivities. They see black leaders like Bill Cosby who publicly address values and social norms within the community as pushing "respectability politics," an accusation that always associates virtuous conduct with seeking acceptance from the white majority. The preoccupation with the thoughts, words, and deeds of white people is common among modern Afristocrats, in large part because they believe that whites are both the cause and cure for the negative social outcomes in black America.

One example of this dynamic was the NAACP's 2020 PSA featuring several white actors pledging to "take responsibility" for how they perpetuated racism, either via silence or inaction.[12] It is easy to understand why the entertainers were eager to use their "privilege" to signal their opposition to racism a few weeks after the death of George Floyd. What is far more difficult to comprehend is why one of the oldest civil rights organizations in the country believed that white actors in Hollywood had the power to do *anything* to improve the lives of black people thousands of miles from Rodeo Drive. The unfortunate answer is quite simple: The progressives powering the Afristocracy function as the moral leaders and spiritual guides of white liberals, not the black masses. The PSA captured the symbiotic relationship between black liberals seeking empathy and restitution for sins they didn't endure and white liberals seeking forgiveness and absolution for sins they didn't commit. This dynamic explains why, for example, Michael Eric Dyson appeared on Tucker Carlson's Fox News show in 2017 to encourage whites to give reparations to atone for their privilege and cure racial inequality.[13]

The black leaders of old knew how to balance external critiques of racism and discrimination with internal rebukes of sloth and intemperance. They were cultural physicians who took their duties very seriously. Today's Afristocrats ignore marriage and family structure because they reject attempts to address individual behavior and community standards—but only when those appeals are directed at a black audience. Their focus on "treating" white people shows they practice a very different form of "medicine," a change in priorities that explains the declining health of the black family since the 1960s.

A Different Type of Doctor

Michael Eric Dyson's connection to the Afristocracy extends beyond coining the term and—according to my definition—being one of its archetypical members. He also offers clear examples of *how* black elites avoid talking about the decline of marriage and intact families. To put it simply, Afristocrats reject their role as cultural physicians in favor of being spin doctors. The main purpose of a spin doctor—whether in a private company or the public square—is damage control and reputation management. Spin doctors believe they serve their clients by telling critics that a situation isn't as bad as they think it is. The spin doctors within the Afristocracy are no different. They use distraction, blame-shifting, and deflection to hide—or explain—obvious symptoms of cultural decay. One of their tactics for minimizing serious issues is noting how prevalent they are in the white community. For example, when someone brings up the fact that homicide is the leading cause of death among young black men, spin doctors smugly respond, "Why don't we talk about white-on-white crime?"[14] To spin doctors, rebutting racist stereotypes is far more important than addressing the racial disparities in homicide victimization. The fear of reinforcing stereotypes also keeps spin doctors from honestly addressing the state of the black family, especially the fact that nearly 70 percent of black children are born to unmarried parents.[15]

During a 2013 appearance on MSNBC, Michael Eric Dyson responded to a panelist who cited that statistic by asking about the "pathology" in the white family.[16] Dyson named methamphetamine addiction and "crass materialism" as problems facing white families, but his reason for doing so was not a genuine desire to address the serious challenges facing his fellow citizens. An article in *The Root* that year entitled "Single Parents Aren't the Problem" ran the same play. The author, a professor at Howard University named Ivory A. Toldson, noted that the percentage of black children in single-parent homes is twice the percentage of white children, before adding that "in the context of social impact, total incidents are unequivocally more important than within group percentages."[17] Somehow, this logic is never applied to fatal police shootings or any other outcome where accusations of systemic racism are based on disparate rates, not raw numbers. Spin doctors want all the attention on black people when talking about racial victimization but deflect it for any social outcome that requires individual agency. The highest form of cultural betrayal to a spin doctor is when a black person says something critical, but true, about black people or culture. They typically respond to those types of critiques by refocusing attention on systemic issues or institutions controlled by whites.

The second common tactic spin doctors use to avoid uncomfortable truths is to minimize the importance of the issue being discussed. Michael Eric Dyson delivered a masterclass in this deflection technique during an MSNBC roundtable on the "myth of the magical black father" that dismissed the importance of marriage and family structure. At one point in the discussion, Dyson stated that "we want healthy families, not nuclear families," noting that "anything nuclear is bound to react ultimately anyway."[18] He continued his focus on the potential for domestic violence when a father is in the home instead of noting that decades of research demonstrate that children raised by their married biological parents do better across numerous social and economic indicators than children raised in other family arrangements.[19]

Likewise, Harvard sociologist Christina J. Cross's 2025 book *Inherited Inequality: Why Opportunity Gaps Persist Between Black and White Youth Raised in Two-Parent Families* attempts to minimize the importance of of the nuclear family. Cross acknowledges that children raised in two-parent homes have better social outcomes compared with those raised by a single parent but argues that black children raised by both parents do not benefit from that family structure as much as their white counterparts. She states that "rather than being a Great Equalizer, the two-parent family, is in fact, a Great Distracter."[20] For Cross, improving life outcomes for black children requires two things. One is eliminating racist policies and social norms that limit opportunities for upward mobility for African Americans. The other is increasing government spending on social welfare programs like TANF and WIC to address the disparities in financial resources that currently exist between black and white households. The main takeaway of *Inherited Inequality* is that when it comes to black families, a payment from the state is more valuable than the presence of a father. Or to put it another way: Black dads don't matter.

Greg Carr, a professor of Afro-American Studies at Howard University, used the weight of history to take the Afristocracy's cultural malpractice even further. He appeared on Roland Martin's news program in 2021 to discuss the Texas law banning abortions after a baby's heartbeat could be detected—typically around six weeks of pregnancy. He drew a connection between the new law and slavery by claiming that black women leaving the state to seek abortions would be recreating "an approximation of the Underground Railroad" with the support of people helping them flee to "civilized states to terminate pregnancies."[21] It is hard to imagine African American elites in previous generations claiming that killing black babies in utero is an act of liberation or political resistance, but this is par for the course among the modern Afristocracy.

Another way spin doctors deflect and dismiss issues is by claiming that people can't see the truth because they are blinded by racial stereotypes. An op-ed from *New York Times* columnist Charles M. Blow entitled "Black Dads Are Doing Best of All" reflects this common tactic. Blow starts his opinion piece by noting that nearly 72 percent of black women who gave birth in 2013 were unmarried. He claims that people who promote the marriage-before-carriage approach to family formation are somehow suggesting "black fathers are pathologically prone to desertion of their offspring and therefore largely responsible for black community 'dysfunction.'"[22] Blow goes on to cite a 2013 CDC study on father involvement that has been used regularly over the past decade to refute the types of entrenched narratives he mentions in his column, specifically that black men are absent, uninvolved dads. The study found that among fathers who lived with their young children, black dads (78 percent) were more likely to eat meals with their children every day than white dads (74 percent) or Hispanic dads (64 percent).[23] Similarly, high levels of involvement were found among black fathers compared with their peers with respect to bathing, reading, and playing with their children.

These findings surprised many people, especially those who are not familiar with the complexities of black family life. For example, you can see black fathers doing drop-offs and pickups at daycare centers and elementary schools every day in low-income neighborhoods across the country, even though most are not married to the mother of their child. The issue with the study wasn't the findings. The problem was how people used it primarily for the purpose of "correcting" narratives rather than understanding the real challenges facing black families. While it's true that the study showed that black fathers who lived with their children were more active in their children's lives than their counterparts in other races, what matters most is that one phrase: "lived with their children." The study showed depressing numbers for those who did not live with their children. For example, only 8 percent of all fathers in the study who lived apart from their young children ate with them every day, while 43 percent said they didn't eat with their children at all and 27 percent said they did so once a week.[24] Non-resident fathers across ethnic lines also seem to become less involved as their children get older. Only 3 percent of non-resident fathers with children ages 5–18 ate with them every day.[25] More than 50 percent didn't eat with their kids at all, and 32 percent did so once a week.[26]

Though black fathers who didn't live with their children were found to be more involved than their white and Hispanic counterparts, the problem is that 44 percent of all black children live apart from their fathers, a percentage far higher than any other group.[27] That means that there are millions of black children who have sporadic and unpredictable contact—if any—with their dads. Charles Blow's selective use of the study thus produced more obscuring smoke than it did clarifying light. An apples-to-apples comparison that examines fathers of all races who live with their children makes black fathers look good by comparison, as does an oranges-to-oranges comparison of fathers of all races who do not live with their children. The problem is when it comes to black family life on the whole, there are many more oranges than there are apples.

Though a father residing with his children doesn't necessarily mean the father is married to the mother, the percentage of children living with two *unmarried* parents is in the single digits across every ethnic group. [28] That means the best way to ensure that more children grow up with active, involved fathers is to promote marriage as the cornerstone of family life. This is an important point, but it will never be addressed by spin doctors more concerned with image management than healing the home.

Racial spin doctors give the impression they care about black people, but they are far more concerned with defying social norms and refuting stereotypes than finding a cure for chronic social maladies. One of the reasons Michael Eric Dyson and his fellow progressive spin doctors resented Bill Cosby's public comments about self-destructive cultural practices is because they think the worst part of having dirty laundry is airing—not wearing—it.

Political Self-Destruction

Many would agree that the elitist leadership models of past generations do not work today. But to the extent that any community, culture, or country has people who educate children, manage resources, administer government, and influence public sentiment, it is better for those people to be godly, competent, and wise. Unfortunately, modern Afristocrats have become agents of intellectual destruction and moral compromise. They have allowed the traditional family to disintegrate because they seem far more interested in lecturing white people than leading black people.

There was a time when black leaders across the political spectrum would speak publicly about the importance of intact, two-parent homes. The Rev. Jesse Jackson expressed great concern about the state of the black community in a special discussion after the airing of *The Vanishing Family* in 1986. He described the phenomenon of young men and women creating multiple children with different partners as a problem of "moral degeneracy." Unlike many Afristocrats today, he believed that poor black people could actually exercise agency over their own lives. Eleanor Holmes Norton echoed Jackson's perspective in the same discussion. Norton has represented the District of Columbia in the US House of Representatives for more than thirty years. She was a contributor to the *Black Women's Manifesto* in the 1970s. She also wrote an essay entitled "Restoring the Traditional Black Family" for *The New York Times Magazine* in 1985. It is hard to imagine a feminist professor or politician writing the same thing today. It is even harder to imagine *The New York Times* publishing it.

The most prominent black leader to directly address marriage and family structure in the past forty years has been President Barack Obama. He did it when he campaigned for president in 2007 and on several occasions during his two terms in office, including during a speech in Chicago on strengthening the middle class, given a few days after his 2013 State of the Union address. There, he spoke at length about the scourge of violent crime in many poor and working-class neighborhoods, and, as he often did, connected it to the family.

> There's no more important ingredient for success, noth-
> ing that would be more important for us reducing violence,
> than strong, stable families—which means we should do
> more to promote marriage and encourage fatherhood. Don't
> get me wrong—as the son of a single mom who gave ev-
> erything she had to raise me with the help of my grand-
> parents, I turned out okay . . . But at the same time, I wish
> I had had a father who was around and involved.[29]

President Obama's concern about violence in Chicago was genuine, especially considering a tragedy that had occurred only weeks
earlier. A fifteen-year-old high school student named Hadiya Pen-
dleton had been killed in a shooting in Chicago. The murder of
any person is unconscionable, but this one struck a personal chord
with the president. Not only was Hadiya's high school within walking distance of the Obamas' family home on the city's South Side,
but she was killed only eight days after she performed with her
high school's marching band at the president's second inaugura-
tion.

During his speech in Chicago, the president told the audience
how he talked about the loss of Hadiya during his State of the
Union Address and informed them that Michelle Obama had attended her funeral. So when Obama made the case that stable
families reduce violence, he surely had Hadiya in mind. But not
everyone was pleased with the president's message about marriage
and fatherhood, despite data backing his claims. Brittney Cooper
wrote in *EBONY* magazine that she found herself "deeply in-
censed" at President Obama's promotion of marriage and strong
families as solutions to community violence.[30] Cooper was livid at
Obama's words and unmoved by the broader context of his remarks. She felt he was promoting narratives about broken homes

and absent dads, and, like many spin doctors, she tried to deflect the real issue of violence by bringing up white males who've carried out mass shootings. Her dismissive attitude toward the importance of family structure and fathers should surprise no one, but the fact that her public rebuke was published in *EBONY* magazine was significant.

EBONY was founded in 1942 by John H. Johnson, whose publishing company was headquartered in Chicago. *EBONY* and its sister magazine *Jet* targeted an African American audience and focused on news, culture, and entertainment. The two magazines amplified the work of the civil rights movement in the 1960s, including *Jet*'s decision to publish a photo of Emmett Till after his brutal murder in 1955.

But *EBONY* was more than just a magazine. It was a brand that reflected the aspirations of black Americans who wanted better lives for themselves and their families in the only country they had ever known. The magazine even featured Barack and Michelle Obama on more than a dozen covers, with headlines that included "America's Next First Couple" and "Celebrate Black Love." The Afristocracy gushed over stories that painted the Obamas as the prototypical black power couple.

Yet even the Obamas were not immune when they attempted to speak of the tie between family structure and social outcomes. This anti-family ideology is so prevalent that a magazine known for promoting racial uplift rebuked the first black president for promoting marriage and intact households. Black leaders in the early part of the twentieth century used their institutions and resources to uplift the race, including by addressing issues of morality, character, and conduct. Black elites today generally do not, especially on issues related to the family. This code of silence underscores the difference in worldview between the black masses who understand the importance of marriage and black elites who use their status to undermine the institution.

Black conservatives have been consistent about the importance of family structure for decades. It's black *progressives* who have changed their tune, largely because the Democratic Party demands they focus more on who is in the White House than what is going on in the home. It is no coincidence that Obama was the last prominent Democratic politician willing to consistently connect family structure and social outcomes. Every black leader since then knows that if the first black president can be attacked for promoting the family, then the progressives in media and academia will be even more vicious with them. The most visible and influential black institutions and spokespeople all espouse a political worldview that is, at best, center-left. This includes the politicians, media companies, civil rights organizations, journalists, entertainers, religious figures, and business leaders who form the modern Afristocracy. These are the people who must be engaged and persuaded to reorder their priorities—by any means necessary—if a movement to rebuild the black family is to have any chance of succeeding. This is not an easy assignment and will require people to speak with courage, clarity, and conviction. Only time will tell if there are any black leaders up to the task.

Conclusion

Doctors study the human body for years. They are trained to observe symptoms, make a diagnosis, recommend a treatment, and give a prognosis. They understand how the physical environment, individual choices, and family history interact to produce specific health outcomes. The entire point of their work is to see their patients get healthy, whether that means giving vaccines for prevention, antibiotics for cure, or medication for chronic conditions that will never go away. Some may not have the ideal bedside manner, preferring blunt honesty to gentle dialogue. This does not mean they dislike their patients or are insensitive to health factors beyond their control. The physician's job is to recommend the course of treatment that is most likely to be effective, regardless of the patient's circumstances or willingness to admit he is sick.

One of the reasons changes in social norms and public policy have had such harmful effects on the black family is that a subtle, yet fundamental, shift has occurred in the purpose and priorities of the cultural physicians who form the modern black leadership class. The social pathogens of big government and feminism made the black family sick, but the neglect of black leaders allowed the condition to get worse. Afristocrats have no problem telling people how to think, speak, and behave—as long as the audience is white.

One of the easiest and most effective steps black leaders and cultural influencers can take is to simply preach what they practice. One reason the "Who's Your Daddy" mobile DNA testing truck stayed busy in New York City is because our society has rejected the marriage-before-carriage model of family formation. But make no mistake, that truck is unlikely to find its way to Martha's Vineyard. The Afristocrats who summer there have built lives that are a testament to hard work, focus, and dedication. They may defend destructive social norms on cable news shows, but there is no way they are telling their own daughters that a woman who has five children with her husband is the same as one who has five children by five different men.

Why is it so difficult to break progressives out of their penchant for talking "left" but living "right"? One reason is because they have believed the lie that any discussion of agency and responsibility pertaining to black people is tantamount to "blaming the victim." They have spent decades arguing that the only things holding blacks back are economic inequality and systemic racism. That may help them sell books to guilty and gullible liberals, but the black family will never be restored to its rightful place if the only solutions Afristocrats can offer are bigger government and better white people.

FIVE

Distort the Bible
for Political Power

In 2008, during his first run for president, Senator Barack Obama attended a candidate forum with megachurch pastor Rick Warren. The conversation was broadcast on CNN and touched on several subjects, including the economy, faith, abortion, stem-cell research, and the war in Iraq. At one point in the conversation, Warren asked the first-term senator to define marriage. Obama stated he believed "marriage is the union between a man and a woman," adding that "for me as a Christian, it is also a sacred union. God's in the mix."[1] Warren followed up by asking whether he would support a constitutional amendment with that definition. Obama said he would not, stressing that the issue should be left for states to decide.[2] At the time only one state—Massachusetts—legally recognized same-sex marriages.

The entire exchange was a microcosm of the broader cultural and political climate in the country. Obama stated that he was not someone who "promotes same-sex marriage" but did voice his support for civil unions. He concluded that part of the conversation by stating that his faith was strong enough to accommodate changes to the legal definition of marriage. Obama spoke like a man trying to appease moderates while affirming both the gay couples in his personal life and his commitment to the civil rights legacy of his party.

It took only one election cycle for Obama to revise his opinion on the issue of marriage and declare it publicly. In an interview with ABC News on May 9, 2012, President Obama—who was facing Mitt Romney in his bid for re-election—stated that he felt it was "important for me to go ahead and affirm that I think same-sex couples should be able to get married."[3] His change of heart was not without some ideological concession, however, given his acknowledgement that "the word marriage is something that provokes very powerful traditions and religious beliefs."[4] Indeed, Obama's statement was radical. For roughly two thousand years, every mainstream Christian denomination held the view that marriage was reserved for one man and one woman.

From there, the mainstream press framed gay marriage as a civil rights issue. Within one week of Obama's ABC appearance, a coalition of black ministers and civil rights leaders released an open letter embracing the president's position on what was being hailed as "marriage equality":

> Dr. Martin Luther King, Jr. once said, "Injustice anywhere is a threat to justice everywhere." As leaders in today's Civil Rights Movement, we stand behind the President Obama's [sic] belief that same sex couples should be allowed to join in civil marriages.[5]

This coalition included Rev. Al Sharpton of the National Action Network; Julian Bond, Chairman Emeritus of the NAACP; and Rev. Dr. Joseph Lowery, a civil rights icon and close Obama ally. The letter also noted that individuals could have different views on the issue but still work toward a set of "common goals," including "fair housing and equitable education, affordable health care and eradicating poverty."[6]

Another impassioned Christian defense of same-sex marriage came from Rev. Otis Moss III, pastor of Trinity United Church of Christ in Chicago—the church Barack Obama attended prior to his public split from Rev. Jeremiah Wright in 2008. Moss read a letter to his church shortly after Obama's public about-face on same-sex marriage. The note, which was sent to a fellow clergyman, started by stating that when ministers "make biblical claims without sound interpretation we run the risk of adopting a doctrinal position of deep conviction but devoid of love."[7]

This conflict between doctrine and love is a consistent theme in Moss's letter. His closing goes even further, implying that doctrine can even prove the enemy of love. As examples of those who put "doctrine over love," he cites the perpetrators of two infamous racist hate crimes:

> Emmitt [*sic*] Till and the four little girls who were assassinated in Alabama during worship did not die for a Sunday sermonic sound bite to show disdain for one group of God's people. They were killed by an evil act enacted by men who believed in doctrine over love . . . Do not let the rhetoric of this debate keep you from the polls, my friend.[8]

Moss weaponized these horrors to justify moving away from the traditional teaching on marriage that had been accepted by all Christians for nearly two thousand years. He was one of the first prominent pastors to publicly support the redefinition of marriage, but he would not be the last.

In 2022, President Joe Biden codified the Supreme Court's *Obergefell* decision legalizing same-sex marriage nationwide when he signed the Respect for Marriage Act into law. Senator Raphael Warnock issued a statement of approval on the bill after it passed in the Senate a few weeks earlier:

> Every human being has inherent dignity and it's crucial that Congress guarantees the right for people to marry whoever they love. I'm proud to support protecting marriage equality rights for all—something that is far overdue.[9]

Warnock's response was particularly noteworthy because, in addition to being a federal lawmaker, he is also the pastor of Ebenezer Baptist Church in Atlanta—the same congregation Rev. Dr. Martin Luther King led in the 1960s.

Obama, Moss, and Warnock drew the same conclusion about the biblical meaning of marriage: It harms the oppressed and marginalized. Today, the black pastors who are reliable surrogates for the Democratic Party every election cycle have followed their lead. They have adopted a new perspective on marriage that better serves their political goals. The progressive Christian movement has sacrificed the God-ordained foundation of the family for a political agenda. To put it more plainly, these ministers have prioritized the White House over the black family. That means that the black church has become a liability, not an asset, in efforts to strengthen the family. The church can't possibly aid in rebuilding the family if it is unwilling to preach with biblical clarity and conviction about sex and marriage. It is ironic that in wielding their religious authority to push for progressive political priorities, the same preachers who claim to bring freedom to the oppressed have become slaves to their own ideology.

It has not always been this way. The black church has been a beacon of hope, moral formation, and spiritual regeneration when the nation has been in crisis. In order to see how lost it has become, we first need to appreciate its crucial historical role.

The Roots and Role of the Black Church

The black church has been bound up with a desire for political freedom—and understandably so—since the beginning. Much like the black family itself, the history of the black church is directly linked to American chattel slavery. While some enslaved Africans brought their Christian faith with them, the spread of Christianity among slaves in America was largely through missionaries and evangelists.[10] The biblical theme of liberation had a special significance to Christian slaves, particularly God's deliverance of the Israelites from Egyptian bondage.[11] This inspiration was expressed in spirituals such as "Go Down, Moses," which includes God's command to the Hebrew prophet to "tell old Pharaoh, let my people go."[12] Christianity was widespread among slaves by the middle of the nineteenth century, including both regular Sunday worship in the local church and secret prayer meetings in slave cabins.[13] The former was seen by slaves as a tool for making them more accepting of their social position. One former slave, Charlie Van Dyke, recounted:

> Church was what they called it but all that preacher talked about was for us slaves to obey our masters and not to lie and steal. Nothing about Jesus, was ever said and the overseer stood there to see the preacher talked as he wanted him to talk.[14]

The truncated biblical teaching slaves heard during formal services created a longing for a more authentic expression of their faith. This led to clandestine meetings where slaves could sing, pray, and worship as they desired. These unsanctioned gatherings came at great risk. Slaves could be whipped if they were caught attending illicit prayer meetings.[15] Moses Grandy, a former slave who became an author and abolitionist, reported that his brother-in-law Isaac, "was flogged, and his back pickled" for preaching at a secret service in the woods.[16]

With time, the realities of race and racism led to the formation of new denominations. Richard Allen was a former slave and Methodist minister who left his predominantly white church in 1787 because it segregated black congregants.[17] He founded the first black Protestant denomination, the African Methodist Episcopal (AME) Church, in the early 1800s.[18] Several other black Protestant denominations were founded before the turn of the century, including the African Methodist Episcopal Zion (AME Zion) Church in 1821, the Christian Methodist Episcopal (CME) Church in 1870, the National Baptist Convention, USA, Inc., in 1880, and the Church of God in Christ (COGIC) in 1897.[19]

From the earliest days of their work as ministers, black preachers were concerned about both the spiritual needs and social condition of the African American community. In an essay published in 1902 entitled "To What Extent Is the Negro Pulpit Uplifting the Race?," Rev. John B. L. Williams observed the effect the Christian faith had on free blacks, some of whom were born into slavery.

> From these pulpits the Gospel goes forth with simplicity
> and power. Its truth and teaching is made to touch, shape
> and direct the practical side of Christian life. The evils
> which exist and which are a menace to the best and purest

modes of life are strongly denounced and openly rebuked by the Negro Christian pulpit, and the race is being led to understand that sound moral character is the foundation upon which to build a strong, symmetrical, well-rounded manhood.[20]

Other pastors applied their biblical training to the political and civic spheres. Bishop B. W. Arnett was an AME preacher who was elected to the Ohio state legislature in 1885 from a district with a white majority.[21] He played a key role in overturning the state's discriminatory "Black Laws." As Rev. Williams noted in his essay, black ministers serving in elected office and various civic capacities were completely normal during this period. He put the leadership role of black preachers in helpful historical context when he declared, "Now as in the past, the Negro pulpit constitutes the true leadership of the race."[22]

This leadership role continued well into the 1960s, where black ministers—most notably Dr. King—were at the forefront of the civil rights movement. Given the legal barriers to full social and political equality facing black Americans in the 1950s, it is easy to understand why civil rights were a frequent topic in the sermons of Dr. King and other black preachers in the Jim Crow era. Racial discrimination was embedded in American law and social custom. That does not mean ministers were blind to other issues. Dr. King's analysis of the issues facing families in the 1950s indicates he saw a clear connection between home life and cultural stability.

The tragic disintegration of the modern family also means the possible loss of our national security. Family life is still the basic unit of the life of the nation, and on healthy family life depends the moral and spiritual life of the nation . . . The relentless lesson of history cannot be escaped, and that is when the family structure begins to break down the structure of the nation itself begins to crack and crumble.[23]

While Dr. King's comments about family were as prophetic as anything he wrote about race, the civil rights work that made him an iconic figure continued the long tradition of black preachers weaving biblical themes of freedom and justice into their public expressions of faith.

Parallel to King's leadership ran the more radical, revolutionary black liberation movement. From that movement emerged a new understanding of freedom that permeates black churches to this day, with devastating effects.

How the Black Church Lost Its Religion

While Dr. King is commonly credited with setting the direction for the black church's engagement in American civic and political life, there's one figure whose influence is far greater. The person with the most lasting influence on progressive preachers today is Dr. James Cone, the father of black liberation theology. His ideas clearly prioritized political activism over biblical fidelity.

Cone's theology continues to shape the thinking of African American pastors regarding the purpose of the Christian faith, the role of the black church, and the duties of the black preacher. Cone believed that in a "revolutionary situation," theology is never neutral and is either "identified with those who inflict oppression or with those who are its victims."[24] In his 1970 book *A Black Theology of Liberation,* he states:

> Insofar as Black Theology is a theology arising from an identification with the oppressed black community and seeks to interpret the gospel of Jesus Christ in the light of the liberation of that community, it is Christian theology. American white theology is a theology of the Antichrist, insofar as it arises from an identification with the white community, thereby placing God's approval on white oppression of black existence.[25]

Dr. Cone developed his liberation theology at the height of the Black Power movement, and his ideas appealed to people who lived through Jim Crow segregation. In his book *For My People: Black Theology and the Black Church,* Cone claimed black churches and ministers could have done more to incorporate Marxism to analyze and critique both capitalism and racism.[26] The evolving priorities of black churches in subsequent decades prove Cone's theological framework has a much wider application than income inequality and racial discrimination. His teachings explain why modern-day black ministers abandon Christian doctrine on sex, sexuality, and marriage whenever a new "marginalized" group feels the Bible is aiding in their oppression.

There is nothing unbiblical about people in bondage being drawn to Christian teaching on freedom and liberty, as many former slaves were. Cone's great error is the idea that political liberation is the chief aspect of God's character. Much like the "prosperity gospel" guarantees material flourishing, liberation theology distorts the Gospel by transforming Jesus into a spiritual genie whose main purpose is to free his followers from political oppression. The genesis of the black church's institutional compromise was a different flavor of "prosperity preaching," with "social justice" as the desired goal instead of material wealth. The preachers who abandoned biblical truth in the face of political pressure to advocate for new victim groups use a subtle yet effective three-part process to make theological rebellion look like a biblical imperative.

First, liberation theologians believe that freedom from social and economic inequality, rather than sin, is mankind's greatest need. Second, they hitch additional oppression categories (e.g., sexuality, gender identity) to the civil rights movement, bestowing new victim groups with the moral authority and cultural capital to fight their "oppressors." Finally, they bypass clear biblical texts that address whatever social transformation new oppressed groups are seeking in favor of unrelated passages, political talking points, folk wisdom, and clichés that give their support a veneer of spiritual authority. This is why preachers like Al Sharpton, Otis Moss III, and Raphael Warnock were willing to suppress Bible verses on marriage that impeded the left's fight for "marriage equality" in favor of a "love is love" mantra that was easier to fit into a civil rights template that made *gay* the new *black*. In fact, in public remarks after the release of his 2011 book, *The Cross and the Lynching Tree*, Cone compared churches that did not fully affirm queer people to racists who lynched black people.[27]

The theological drift that is a feature of Cone's teaching has made many politically engaged black pastors ambivalent to efforts to strengthen the family. Progressive pastors steeped in liberation theology *can't* preach with biblical clarity and conviction about sex, marriage, and family because doing so would be seen as an act of violence against groups they believe are marginalized. They also feel political pressure from a Democratic Party that speaks the language of racial justice and has successfully branded itself as the chief defender of black progress and civil rights.

This has led to a fusion of racial solidarity and political loyalty that creates the illusion that "voting blue" is the "black" choice for socially conscious African Americans. This cultural reality has trapped many black pastors in an ideological box. They claim to be brave prophets willing to speak truth to power, but they are more like cupbearers for the left—there to serve, not challenge, the people in charge.

These religious leaders need to be set free from the theological and political shackles that keep them bound. Only then will they be able to affirm the reality that, whether a person believes the Bible or just in biology, there are only two sexes—male and female. This statement would have been unnecessary fifty years ago but needs to be defended in a culture that promotes the idea that sex is assigned at birth, gender is a social construct, and a person can switch genders—or have no gender at all—based on what they feel on the inside. Genesis 1:27 (ESV) is a foundational verse for family restoration because it speaks to both the source of human worth and the sex binary: "So God created man in his own image, in the image of God he created him; male and female he created them." Biblical fidelity would also require black pastors to tell political leaders that the blueprint for marriage is found in Genesis 2:24 (ESV): "Therefore a man shall leave his father and his mother and hold fast to his wife, and they shall become one flesh." The one-flesh nature of the marital union is essential to its purpose, but those who have sought to redefine marriage through both law and culture reject this biblical truth.

Progressives are quick to note the diversity of family structures that exist in society, but the fact remains that it still takes one man and one woman to create a baby. Marriage exists to recognize, affirm, and bless the union between a man and woman precisely because it is the only relationship arrangement that produces children. The reason societies have traditionally accorded special status and support to marriage is because the one-flesh union between husband

and wife is designed, in principle, for procreation. Exceptions to this rule don't negate the fact that without significant and willful scientific manipulation, it is the relationship between one man and one woman that naturally makes a child. Society has good reason to respect, recognize, and protect this relationship because it is so distinct from every other.

Restoring order in the home requires getting back to the basics about sex, marriage, and family. Unfortunately, far too many black pastors have fallen away from biblical teaching on these issues and abandoned the role the church has traditionally played in African American life.

A Devil's Bargain

If the priorities of progressive pastors were in order, they would speak biblical truth to the political party their members help put into power. Instead, liberation theology has transformed the black church from a religious institution dedicated to the pursuit of righteousness to the religious wing of the Democratic Party. This is the devil's bargain that liberation-minded black preachers and churches struck with progressives on issues that are directly linked to the family. They traded biblical fidelity for the *appearance* of social justice. The clearest example of political preachers making this pivot was after President Obama came out in support of same-sex marriage. By affirming his stance—or remaining silent on the issue—they abrogated their biblical authority and ceded the debate about marriage to the political sphere. This prevents them from addressing family matters with biblical and moral clarity, an act of theological malpractice that extends beyond marriage to undermine other aspects of family life, including abortion and gender roles.

A 2022 *Washington Post* article entitled "Why Some Black Churches Aren't Elated About the Possible End of *Roe*" shows that even the destruction of black babies can be justified when abortion restrictions are framed as tools of oppression.[28] Multiple clergymen talked about being personally pro-life in theological terms but not political terms. One was Rev. Cheryl Sanders, senior pastor of the Third Street Church of God in Washington, DC. Leaving aside the fact that the Bible reserves the pastoral office—marked by the responsibility to teach and exercise authority over the church— for qualified men, Rev. Sanders' perspective on abortion is a sign of deep distress for many black churches. The article noted she "doesn't want to align herself with far-right conservative activists she disagrees with on many social issues."[29]

Another black minister in DC stated that conservatives "don't care about Black babies" because they had a different perspective on how the Voting Rights Act should be applied in today's political landscape.[30] Other ministers cited fatal police incidents and funding for historically black colleges and universities (HBCUs) as more pressing concerns than abortion. One pastor interviewed for the article, Earle J. Fisher of Abyssinian Missionary Baptist Church in Memphis, was a member of Planned Parenthood's Clergy Advocacy Board. The article put the fusion of race, religion, and politics in stark terms: "While Black churchgoers share religious values with White Christians, their racial identity, along with historical distrust over issues such as civil rights, has made it more difficult to come together."[31]

When *Roe* was finally overturned a month later in the *Dobbs v. Jackson* case, black pastors were some of the loudest critics of the

Supreme Court's ruling. Pastor Howard-John Wesley of Alfred Street Baptist Church donned an "I'm With Her" shirt after the decision and scolded pro-life Christians who didn't attend Black Lives Matter protests.[32] Wesley is a Cone disciple who leads a popular and influential church for educated, politically conscious upper-middle-class African Americans in the DC area. The Obamas attended his Easter service on more than one occasion while they occupied the White House, and the church made a $1 million donation to the National Museum of African American History and Culture.[33]

Jamal Bryant, pastor of New Birth Missionary Baptist Church in Atlanta, criticized the decision and said a true "pro-life" culture would have stricter gun laws and provide greater access to food. He stood on stage and declared that "women have the right to have authority over their body." Then he performed a baby dedication, declaring "children are our future" before pivoting back to his normal pro-abortion talking points—apparently unaware of, or at least unconcerned about, the contradiction.[34] Bryant is noteworthy for another reason. His 2025 boycott of Target over its rollback of corporate diversity, equity, and inclusion (DEI) initiatives was reminiscent of the black preachers who backed President Obama in 2012 because they thought a fight over marriage would get in the way of their progressive policy priorities. At the time, they mentioned fair housing, equitable education, and eliminating poverty. Today, much of the focus is on those issues as well as fighting back against the Trump administration's policy agenda.

I saw this dynamic of pastors prioritizing politics and policy over family matters when I spoke at Hampton University's annual black family conference in 2025. The audience was receptive to my talk entitled "The Black Family Blueprint," but one of the earlier panels on the black church was noteworthy for how little the clergy members talked about the institution of marriage. The first question to the panel was how "white theology" differs from "black theology" and how the latter can be used for the purpose of "liberation." Much of the conversation focused on standard progressive policy concerns. There were references to food deserts, home ownership, health outcomes, and opposing the Trump administration's dismantling of DEI and affirmative action. The first mention of the word "marriage" occurred during the Q&A portion of the session, not from the panelists, but when I asked the panelists whether they defined the institution biblically. They all said yes, but they also stated that the church should be "sensitive" to the culture and not too dogmatic. Other feedback included the belief we can't "legislate morality" and that the church has to "earn the right" to speak the truth when it comes to issues of sex and sexuality.

Their comments were not surprising. The black preachers who see themselves in the mold of James Cone have used their pulpits to draw the church further away from biblical teaching on the most important issues related to the family, including the reality of biological sex, the definition of marriage, and the sanctity of human life. In turn, the progressives who have been at the forefront of the LGBT and abortion movements see black preachers as valuable spokesmen who lend their causes needed moral authority. These are the pastors journalists have in mind when they talk about the "black church" and the people politicians contact when they want to engage the African American community.

Conclusion

The Christian faith is by nature conservative—in a theological sense. The scriptures are replete with verses pointing to the unchanging and enduring nature of God and the Bible. Revelation 1:8 says, "'I am the Alpha and the Omega,' says the Lord God, 'who is and who was and who is to come, the Almighty.'" Malachi 3:6 says, "For I the Lord do not change; therefore you, O children of Jacob, are not consumed." Isaiah 40:8 says, "The grass withers, the flower fades, but the word of our God will stand forever." Hebrews 13:8 says, "Jesus Christ is the same yesterday and today and forever." These verses do not mean that the biblical text cannot be distorted or manipulated by self-serving people, but it does mean that the Bible is not a party platform that gets updated every four years.

Thankfully, there are countless others who are faithfully preaching and teaching God's word. These congregations are often small and do not receive any media attention. Many are led by pastors more concerned with preparing their members for eternity in heaven than getting souls to the polls on Election Day. Some of these churches have vibrant ministries for men, women, and families. They are committed to remaining faithful to biblical ethics regarding sex, sexuality, marriage, family, and the sanctity of life without any concern for whether elected Democrats—or Republicans— agree. They know that Pride has infiltrated the church and have decided to stand for the cross rather than hide in the closet.

The choice before progressive black pastors, churches, and believers is simple. They must choose between the Bible or their "black card" because racial authenticity has been tethered to a political program that is often at odds with Christian teaching. They can either believe that man's greatest source of bondage is sin or argue that Jesus came to ensure equity for "marginalized people of color." They can either affirm that sex is established at conception or believe that individuals get to choose their own gender according to what they feel on the inside. They can either uphold the inherent value of all life or chant "black lives matter" in solidarity with people who think it is better for a child to be killed in the womb than be born to a poor black mother. They can either accept God's design for marriage—one man and one woman dedicated to one another for one lifetime—or continue to go along with the progressives who will eventually argue that legalizing polyamorous unions is the new civil rights fight of this generation.

Liberation-minded pastors who reject the biblical definitions and descriptions of sex and marriage are incapable of doing the work needed to rebuild the black family. They fashion themselves as brave prophets, but they make race and politics twin idols that draw their hearts—and pulpits—away from God. Christians are often told to beware of wolves in sheep's clothing. That is wise counsel, but what's even more dangerous is a wolf in *shepherd's* clothing. The former can devour a few sheep before the others scatter, but the latter can lead an entire flock over a cliff. One ray of hope is the biblical theme of God's mercy on those who turn from their wicked ways and trust Him. The pattern in both the Old and New Testaments is quite familiar. God's people rebel. He rebukes them. They reflect on their sin and repent. He restores them. This is my prayer, because the black family needs the church to function in its God-given role now more than ever.

A New Era

My focus to this point has been on the institutions and ideas that have either caused or abetted the breakdown of the black family. The first three chapters dealt with the deformation of marriage, the displacement of men, and the deception of women. The next two chapters addressed the black leaders who have stood silent as the traditional family structure that survived more than two hundred years of slavery disappeared one generation after the marriage of big-government liberalism and second-wave feminism.

But there is another way to understand this issue. I would argue that the arc of the black family can also be seen in four overlapping eras that span four hundred years of American history. I have given each era a name that captures that time period's primary impact on—or relationship to—the black family. The beginning and end of each era is marked by a significant development in politics, law, policy, or culture.

The first is the Subjugation Era, which began in 1619 with the arrival of roughly twenty slaves in present-day Hampton, Virginia, near the Jamestown colony that was the first permanent English settlement in the Americas.[1] The system of race-based chattel slavery that evolved over the next two centuries would play a major role in the development of the black family. As I covered in chapter 1, the incompatibility of the two institutions—marriage and slavery—deformed the former because true freedom was impossible under the latter. All the expectations of a marital union, from cohabitation to sexual exclusivity, were subject to the whims of slave owners who had the legal standing to exercise their rights over their "property." That meant an enslaved man couldn't protect his wife in the same way as his white counterparts and an owner could split up a household by selling one spouse to another plantation hundreds of miles away. While slavery continued in parts of the country after President Lincoln issued the Emancipation Proclamation, I use this major milestone in 1863 to mark the end of this era.

Slavery distorted the development and stability of the black family, but it didn't destroy it. In fact, the Stability Era of the black family that began in 1863 and lasted for a hundred years was marked by newly emancipated men and women doing everything they could to put their families back together. The newspaper ads that were digitized by the Last Seen Project show how far ex-slaves were willing to travel to find a long-lost spouse. This era also included outcomes related to marriage and family that stand in stark contrast to social norms that have been firmly entrenched for decades. From 1890 through the 1950s, black men and women married earlier and were more likely to be married by thirty-five than their white peers.[2] The fact that they also had a higher non-marital birth rate during that period shows that family formation norms were complicated, especially against the backdrop of centuries of enslavement. This era ended in the early 1960s as a new zeitgeist took hold and disrupted how men and women saw themselves, each other, sex, marriage, and family.

The Subversion Era that put the black family on its current

course began in 1963 with the publication of Betty Friedan's book *The Feminine Mystique.* The 1960s saw the rise of second-wave feminism and the sexual revolution, the expansion of the welfare state, mass marketing of the birth control pill, and the first no-fault divorce law in the country. These developments in government, culture, media, and medicine led men and women to reconsider their relationships with each other, the roles they play in society and the home, and the responsibilities they have to their children. This set the stage for a parallel family structure to emerge that established the government as the de facto head of household for millions of low-income women. The net effects of such massive social changes were felt by all Americans, but the incentives to discard the marriage-before-carriage cultural norm had an even more pronounced impact on the black family. This era also included the steady rise of nonmarital births in black America, eventually crossing 50 percent in the late 1970s and stabilizing at roughly 70 percent since the late 1990s.[3] The end of this era was ushered in by the passage of the Personal Responsibility and Work Opportunity Reconciliation Act, the welfare reform bill signed into law by President Clinton in 1996.

Since 1996, the black family has been in the Surrender Era and exists in a cultural context where elected officials, scholars, religious leaders, political pundits, and social commentators all accept black children being born to—and raised by—unmarried parents as the norm. Daniel Patrick Moynihan predicted failure to address the disintegration of the black family would lead to a cycle of poverty that would continue to repeat itself. But what is clear after more than sixty years is that the decades-long interaction between policy, political ideology, and personal experience creates cultural norms that also reproduce themselves without any external interference. There is no reason to expect a young woman growing up in a Southeast DC neighborhood with an 80 percent nonmarital birth rate to require a husband before having a child if she was raised by a single mother who herself was raised by a single mother.[4] The same applies to the young man she is dating, who was raised without a father in the home and does not have a single friend who grew up with a married mom and dad. Both lack marriage models on a personal level, but they also live at a time where no one *expects* them to be married before having a child together. They do not hear that message from family or friends. They don't hear it from political leaders or preachers. They don't hear it from podcasters or social commentators. They don't hear it from entertainers or athletes. Black leaders often raise their own children in married two-parent homes but remain silent in the face of a 70 percent nonmarital birth rate for the people they claim to speak—and care—for.

In just a few generations, the marriage culture and family structure that sustained the black community from the Civil War through the civil rights movement went from the norm to the exception. Some people will claim this is all about economics, but that doesn't explain why a former slave would travel hundreds of miles to find his wife after thirty years of separation but a rapper worth $30 million refuses to marry any of the women who have birthed his children. This does not mean there aren't other forces at play, but the reason marriage is down across all ethnic groups is because both sexes no longer see the institution as valuable, desirable, accessible, or indispensable for the purpose of starting a family.

Three generations of subversion and surrender have put the traditional black family on the brink of extinction. And when families break down, communities are soon to follow. There are inner-city neighborhoods across the country where intact families are rare and intractable poverty is common. The violence that often follows makes life hard on the single mothers doing their best to raise children in difficult circumstances. The failing schools only exacerbate the problem, pumping out children who can't read their own diplomas.

The consequences of broken homes are obvious, yet politicians and pundits can muster only half-hearted appeals to fixing the system they claim is the root cause. They declare the importance of every institution but marriage and claim that policy outcomes depend on every social structure but the family. They refuse to admit that the disparities they observe, whether in the schoolhouse or jailhouse, start in the home.

It's as if the leaders who claim to speak for these communities have written off any hope that things can change. They do not hesitate to opine on global affairs and irrelevant political controversies, but they refuse to speak a hard, but necessary, truth: The relationship between a child's mother and father will have a much greater impact on the trajectory of his life than a new government program. In fact, the all-encompassing view of government has functioned as a cultural steroid that has deformed the body politic by increasing the power of elected officials and unelected bureaucrats as the family has atrophied.

But family breakdown is about far more than poverty and policy outcomes. Families are made up of real people who want to feel connected, protected, and respected. So many young women can tell the same story of looking for love in all the wrong places because they were subconsciously trying to fill a father-sized void that began in childhood. At the same time, father-hungry young men so often seek guidance in the streets and continue the cycle of broken homes—spreading their seed but never planting roots with one woman and the children they share, together under the same roof. Some children have gone so long without seeing an intact family that they assume marriage isn't a "black" thing.

Make no mistake: Adults have paid a price for the breakdown of the family as well. The women who claim they don't need a man to raise children are fooling themselves. It takes two to make a baby, and it stands to reason that the same two are needed to raise one. Parenting is rewarding, but it also drains even the most active adult of energy at times. Having a husband releases black women from wearing the crown that many can admit is far too heavy for their heads. Likewise, marriage and children give men a greater sense of purpose and orient them toward the future. Marriage gives women the affection and security they desire and men the respect and support they need.

Talk of honoring "the ancestors" is very common in black culture. It is time to put that rhetoric to the ultimate test. Nothing would do more to demonstrate intergenerational appreciation than creating a culture of marriage and family that shows respect for the past by building for the future. This is a time of choosing. If the status quo remains undisturbed, the nonmarital birth rate may hit 85 percent within thirty years, and 60 percent of black children may end up being raised by a single parent. Our only hope is to exit the era of surrender and enter a new era that breathes life back into the black family. Doing so would provide future generations of black children with the ultimate privilege: the structure and stability that come from being raised by their own married mom and dad in a loving household.

A new era will require a level of discipline, focus, self-reflection, honesty, and moral clarity from black leaders that has not been directed toward any *internal* social cause since the turn of the twentieth century. Every political movement for civil rights and racial justice since the 1960s has put the onus of collective action on external parties, typically elected leaders and the white majority. This is an observation, not a criticism. What's needed today is a Revival Era that restores the institution of marriage as the foundation of black family life. This era will require an acknowledgement of both the problem and the degree to which *we* have lost our way, despite gains in educational attainment, economic power, and political representation. This era also needs black people—both the classes and the masses—to marshal the community's spiritual, social, cultural, economic, and political capital for the sake of the family and future.

As a father, I never expect anyone to care more about my children than I do. The responsibility to provide for them and care for their spiritual, emotional, and personal development ultimately belongs to me and my wife, not a random stranger. This is why revival and restoration of the traditional family will never take place if the black leaders in media, academia, and politics make a habit of asking government agencies and corporations what *they* are doing to solve this problem. Make no mistake, the type of uplift needed for the Revival Era cannot be outsourced.

This type of social transformation is a tall task. There are many complex and interrelated components. There will be naysayers and obstacles—often from self-professed "allies" who claim to care about racial equity and justice. The chapters that follow will tackle these issues and more, but the first step is to rediscover what must be restored. And like every massive building project, that work is impossible without both an architect and a blueprint that ensure what's being built sits on a solid foundation that will stand the test of time.

PART II

• • •

The Blueprint
for Restoration

Reframe the Issue for Key Institutions

I remember when—and how—my wife told me she was pregnant with our first child. She handed me a black box that contained a positive pregnancy test. I gave her the biggest hug as a wave of emotion swept over me. In any other circumstance, a person giving a man a stick they urinated on would be met with disgust. But that test represented our bond as husband and wife as well as the blessing of welcoming a child into this world who carries her parents and ancestors in her very DNA. Her gift was a reminder that the institution of marriage joins a man and woman together as husband and wife and provides the optimal environment for raising a child.

When marriage becomes obsolete, however, fathers are seen as optional, and children are left vulnerable. That is one reason marriage revival and family restoration should be seen as a civil rights issue driven by two truths. The first is that all children have a right to the affection and protection of the man and woman who created them. The second is that the ideal environment for children to exercise this right is in a loving and stable home with their married biological parents.

Unfortunately, when it comes to the family, the default in American culture today is to prioritize the desires of adults over the needs of children. That moral framework is completely inverted. Parents have a duty to make sacrifices to provide for the welfare of their children. No child has a duty to sacrifice his well-being for the sake of his parents, but this is exactly what happens to children on a regular basis.

When adults put the baby carriage before marriage, children are often deprived of the benefits that come with having their mother and father under the same roof. In the case of same-sex adoption or surrogacy, the child is intentionally introduced to an environment that robs them of either maternal or paternal affection for the sake of what adults want. With abortion, babies pay the ultimate price so that their mothers can live the lives they desire without the inconvenience of an unwanted child standing in the way.

No one would suggest starting a national movement to address the home lives of a few thousand children scattered across the country. But the fact that most black children do not have the benefit of living under the same roof with their married parents is an injustice that a new civil rights movement must rectify.

If 70 percent of black children were born with a serious health condition that affected less than 30 percent of white children, every civil rights organization would make addressing that disparity a national priority. Progressive leaders would not rest until they found individuals and institutions to hold accountable. They would do everything in their power to remove the barriers blocking precious black children from reaching their full potential. They would undoubtedly attach their new fight to the civil rights struggles of the past, giving their movement a historical connection to previous battles for racial uplift.

Well, the same activists and organizations need to fight with as much passion *for* the family as they do against racial disparities. If they truly desire black social progress, then reviving marriage and intact families on the South Side of Chicago should be as important to them today as voting rights were in Selma, Alabama, in the 1960s. Previous generations were willing to risk their lives to secure civil and political rights for those who came after them.

Thankfully, marriage revival won't require being beaten bloody while marching over a bridge or being attacked by police dogs.

This fight for justice simply requires a walk down the aisle in front of family and friends to start a new life together. That one decision, combined with the commitment to stay together through thick and thin, will do more to improve the lives of black children than another boycott or protest. The activists who sport neatly coiffed afros and raise clenched fists yet remain silent about how the injustice of broken homes disproportionately harms black children should stop cosplaying as freedom fighters and revolutionaries. Their support for a pro-marriage, pro-family, and pro-life movement would be far more radical in today's culture than any left-wing social justice cause.

Getting our thinking right on "rights" requires rejecting the idea that the desires of adults are more important than the needs of children. In contrast, children do have a basic right to the attention, love, and support of the two people who made them. Fathers and mothers have an obligation to their children because creation and stewardship go hand in hand. This book's argument is that those duties are best carried out when they are involved in a loving, monogamous marriage.

This is why the institutions that claim to care about improving social and economic outcomes for black Americans should be focused on promoting a *culture* of stable marriages and intact families. How? By using their resources and influence to consistently reinforce the idea that marriage is valuable, desirable, accessible, and indispensable for the purpose of forming a family. If racial uplift is truly a goal of legacy civil rights organizations, ensuring every black child has a father and mother in the home should be a higher priority than increasing the number of black representatives in Congress. The same goes for other important institutions.

To put it in terms that fit the theme of this book, a marriage and family culture focused on rebuilding the black family also requires support from three *houses*—the church house, the schoolhouse, and the statehouse. While many stakeholders must answer the call for true revival to take place, this chapter will focus on how the church, K–12 schools and HBCUs, and the government can shape values, norms, and public sentiment to promote a culture of marriage and strong families that protects children.

Church House

While I have been critical of black preachers obsessed with politics in previous chapters, my rebuke is motivated in part by the reality that the church is the most important institution needed to revive a culture of marriage in black America. Black pastors who preach the Gospel and believe their Bible are needed more than ever to boldly declare that God's design for humanity, marriage, and the family are all good. Affirming the Bible is the least black pastors can do to restore the family. If black churches want to create a culture of marriage in their communities, they must also be willing to turn doctrine into practice by helping men and women create and sustain loving marriages and stable families.

One of the best decisions my wife and I made after tying the knot was taking a marriage class at a large church in our area. We married less than eighteen months after we first met and, like many couples, had challenges to work through as newlyweds. Everything from managing our finances to the proper method for folding towels could lead to a disagreement, especially since we hadn't known each other long. That's one reason we signed up for the Homebuilders class and were intrigued by its motto: "Building Your Marriage to Last." There were a dozen couples in our class. Some were newlyweds. Others had more years under their belts. Some had children. Others, like us, did not. A few couples had endured major challenges, including separation and divorce.

Regardless of how we ended up in that class, we all understood that building a marriage that lasts for a lifetime would be difficult work, especially if we didn't feel equipped with all the necessary relationship tools. Perhaps this explains why the married couple leading the class required every participant to memorize the first verse of Psalm 127 (ESV) to set our minds at ease:

Unless the Lord builds the house, those who build it labor in vain. Unless the Lord watches over the city, the watchman stays awake in vain.

That class taught me that every structure reflects the handiwork of its designer. Although the home every couple was trying to build looked different, every marriage has the same *architect*. That remains true even if the people who occupy a home don't know—or think about—the person who made the blueprint. While the Bible provides the best blueprint for marital success, you don't have to be Christian to recognize and benefit from how the institution was designed.

More churches should see a revival movement as an opportunity to reach couples through workshops for married couples like

Homebuilders. They could also offer fellowship opportunities for singles as well as premarital classes for couples who are seriously dating. These efforts would certainly benefit existing members, but they would also provide opportunities to reach and minister to people who otherwise wouldn't attend church. Some might already be living together. Close to 70 percent of Americans believe cohabitation is acceptable even if couples do not have plans to get married, and 59 percent say cohabiting couples can raise children just as well as married couples.[1] These findings suggest some pastors will need to nudge some couples to move from shacking up to settling down.

Pastors also have a role to play in helping their members and the broader culture think biblically about concepts related to relationships and marriage that take on different meanings outside a Christian context. For example, how a single and childless radical feminist handles the idea of gender roles will be very different from a minister with forty years of marriage under his belt. This is one reason a biblical blueprint is needed to teach each member of the family what they are supposed to do in the home.

Recognizing the existence of gender-specific roles may sound regressive, but the truth is that cultural expectations for a man's roles in the home have remained quite consistent. There may be many things a man does for his family, but the minimum he *must* do according to our social norms is provide for the material needs of his household. This isn't a recent trend brought about by technological innovation. The creation account in Genesis shows that Adam was given a job—to work and keep the Garden of Eden—before a wife.[2] The New Testament includes a warning that a Christian man who fails to provide for his family has forsaken his faith.[3] A man's ability to provide is so important that women, regardless of their occupation, generally seek men who earn as much or more than they do. One analysis of US census data found that high-earning women (e.g., lawyers and doctors) tended to marry their economic equals while women in the lower income brackets married men who make more.[4]

In recent decades, the role of provider has become increasingly shared. In 1972, 85 percent of husbands were the sole or primary breadwinner, and 11 percent of households had equal contributions from both spouses.[5] Today, 55 percent of husbands are sole or primary breadwinner, 16 percent of women play the role of provider, and 29 percent of couples share the load.[6] While these figures represent a significant cultural shift, no one *expects* a woman to take care of an adult male and the children they have together.

A husband who takes to social media and declares he does not work because he needs to "find himself" and enjoys depending on his wife can expect to be mocked mercilessly. The same would be true if a viral video showed a man running away from a chaotic scene and leaving his wife and children behind. That's because men, who are larger and stronger on average than women, are also expected to protect their families. This responsibility extends beyond physical security. It also takes the form of a father warning his son about hanging out with certain friends and telling his daughter her new boyfriend is no good.

These two roles—providing and protecting—remain the minimum requirements for every man. Any man who fails to do either should expect criticism from his loved ones and ridicule from society. Women today face a completely different set of societal expectations. Even if wives in previous generations did not use these words, the role they played in the home was to nurture and support a husband and children. And much like their male counterparts, expectations for women that are often attributed to culture have their roots in scripture. The Apostle Paul exhorts older women to, among other things, "train the young women to love their husbands and children" and be keepers of the home—duties he connects directly to their faith.[7] While the Bible never forbids women from working outside the home, decades of feminist indoctrination have trained women to prioritize the demands of their company over the needs of their family. A woman who runs a large, complex organization can expect to be applauded in liberal circles—unless it's her home. Likewise, a teacher who dedicates her life to educating the next generation is seen as a hero—unless her students are her own children.

Pinpointing the roles a woman should play in her home is difficult because our culture resists *any* restrictions, boundaries, requirements, or guidelines on how women should conduct themselves. Saying a man *should* provide for his family is perfectly acceptable in public discourse, but the consistent message from major media outlets and social commentators is that a woman should always put her happiness above the needs of her family. This is why the cultural messages women receive most often are about their rights and freedoms, while men are generally reminded of their duties and obligations. It's no wonder then that *The Atlantic* published a story entitled "How I Demolished My Life" that included an admission that while the author loved her husband, she divorced him because "I felt that he was standing between me and the world, between me and *myself*."[8]

The asymmetrical nature of our societal expectations around gender roles affects every aspect of male–female relationships, especially how different members of the household relate to one another. Nothing ignites a battle of the sexes quicker than someone dropping one word—"submission"—into a discussion about marriage. Even in a church service with professing Christians, the topic is sure to unsettle some listeners because the biblical blueprint for the relationship between husbands and wives sounds regressive in a culture that embraces androgynous egalitarianism. Yet here is Paul in his own words:

> Wives, submit to your own husbands, as to the Lord. For the husband is the head of the wife even as Christ is the head of the church, his body, and is himself its Savior. Now as the church submits to Christ, so also wives should submit in everything to their husbands.[9]

Understanding what the Bible teaches about submission is important because it is easy to dismiss the issue if your archetype is a tyrannical husband controlling the color of his wife's socks and an obsequious wife who barely speaks above a whisper and never expresses her opinion on any topic. Biblical submission is neither. It calls a wife to *voluntarily* yield her will to that of her husband, much as a driver pulls over when an emergency vehicle has its lights flashing and siren blaring. We respect the authority that has been given to first responders and allow their vehicle to proceed, even if we had the green light. This is in stark contrast to a model where the husband *forcibly* makes his wife obey his commands, similar to an MMA fighter who puts an opponent in a chokehold and applies pressure until his foe taps out.

The biblical command for a wife to submit to her husband is clear, but the irony of submission discourse, both in and outside of the church, is that it often neglects the biblical command for husbands to love, nourish, and cherish their wives that comes directly after the instructions to women.[10] This is one reason I am skeptical of men who advocate a Christ-less, self-interested style of submission. You can hear echoes of this mindset when men speak about women as foes to be conquered, not helpmates to be cherished. A man who is his own god and submits to no other authority will never reach his full potential as a husband. A good husband understands that he and his wife are one, which means hurting her, whether through word or deed, is tantamount to hurting himself. A husband with a oneness mindset would never justify infidelity by claiming that he is a "high-value" man who has a right to break his marriage vows just because he is more than six feet tall and has a six-figure salary.

I understand that discussing submission in the context of marriage will offend the modern sensibilities of feminists whose instincts are to disrupt hierarchies and deconstruct social norms to "liberate" the "oppressed" from the domination of their "oppressors." But the Bible doesn't frame the world in a feminist lens. Biblical submission maps out the relationship and duties between a husband and wife who are both made in God's image. It establishes order in the home, which is important because authority comes with responsibilities and temptations—abuse for the person who exercises it and subversion for the one under it.

One reason churches must play an integral role in the rebuilding of the black family is because the breakdown of the family is primarily a *spiritual* problem caused by the rejection of the biblical design for sex and marriage, not an economic problem caused by depressed wages or insufficient job opportunities. True marriage revival is possible only through righting the relationship between men, women, and the God who created the institution.

Schoolhouse

Schools also have a role to play in creating a marriage and family culture. One way they can do so is to introduce students to the "success sequence," the three-step pro-family and anti-poverty plan. Research on millennials born between 1980 and 1984 finds that less than 5 percent ended up in poverty by their mid-thirties if they did three things: finish high school, get a job, and marry *before* having children.[11] These steps are tangible, achievable, and measurable. They are also very useful for students who have not grown up in two-parent, middle-class homes. The success sequence also appears to be popular among parents. One survey found that 68 percent of black parents and 74 percent of parents without a college degree favored teaching the success sequence in public schools.[12]

Some critics will say that schools have no business imposing such "conservative" and "normative" values on children who come from diverse backgrounds and don't all share the same religious traditions and cultural expectations. This might be a compelling argument if schools were not already evangelizing the next generation on matters related to sex and sexuality. Here is an official statement New York City Mayor Eric Adams put out in June 2022 that shows K–12 classrooms are already being used for moral instruction:

> At a time when our LGBTQ+ communities are under increased attack across this country, we must use our education system to educate. The goal is not only for our children to be academically smart, but also emotionally intelligent. Drag storytellers, and the libraries and schools that support them, are advancing a love of diversity, personal expression, and literacy that is core to what our city embraces.[13]

New York City has the largest public school system in the country. Between 2018 and 2022, Drag Queen Story Hour NYC received more than $200,000 in taxpayer funding. One national survey conducted in 2022 found that 71 percent opposed taxpayer funding for Drag Queen Story Hour, so I find it hard to believe the parents of New York City's one million school students were happy about how the Department of Education was spending its time and money.[14]

There are also critics who will say that teaching the success sequence could alienate some children who don't live with a married mom and dad, especially those being raised by single mothers. This is an understandable concern, given the fact that less than 40 percent of black children live with two married parents.[15] But inner-city schools already encourage every student who walks in the door to go to college without fear of offending parents who don't have degrees. All the adults involved in a child's education—from parents to principals—are willing to put feelings aside to introduce students to information that can help them lead productive, fulfilling lives. There is no reason this approach to *promoting* college can't be applied to *describing* a surefire way to stay out of poverty.

The role schools can play in family reconstruction does not stop in the twelfth grade. Efforts to strengthen the black family will also require HBCUs to play a role in creating a culture of marriage. Earlier in this book, I criticized black pastors who attended Hampton University's annual conference on the black family and talked more about politics than marriage. But the fact that the university has been hosting the event since the 1980s speaks volumes about its commitment to the black family. Hampton should serve as a model for other HBCUs that want to host events bringing together scholars, pastors, counselors, entertainers, and other stakeholders working to increase the number of stable marriages and intact families in the black community.

Family-focused HBCUs can do much more than host conferences on marriage. They should be at the forefront of research on how men and women view relationships, gender roles, marriage, and family.

Schools can also cultivate a local marriage culture by using faculty and graduate students in the appropriate disciplines to offer premarital education and counseling services to couples in their surrounding communities. Another idea involves allowing campus grounds and facilities to be used for weddings—with discounts for staff and alumni—as long as participating couples give schools permission to use their wedding photos for on-campus marriage marketing campaigns. This town-and-gown partnership would improve the relationships between universities and their neighbors. It could also help create the ring-by-spring culture that is associated with some southern and conservative colleges. A student group might also be interested in hosting a forum on relationships that includes married couples, especially alumni who met on campus—an event that would require little more than an empty room and a few boxes of pizza.

Some schools may take their ideas even further. An HBCU that is an integral part of its community might consider using its student newspaper to recognize married couples on their anniversaries. Others might consider creating a date-night app that pairs students with couples looking for childcare so they can enjoy an evening out together. Some schools might explore ideas that align with their institutional ethos and campus culture, such as creating sex-segregated dorms and instituting provisions that promote chastity by prohibiting sexual relations outside of marriage.

None of these ideas, in isolation, can rebuild the black family. But, taken together, they can plant the seeds of marriage and family life in the minds of students. Black colleges and universities are important institutions that play a critical role in cultivating future lawyers, doctors, and engineers. There is no reason they can't invest in marriage and family work that also produces future husbands and wives.

Statehouse

Like most people who spend any time on public transportation in New York City, I saw my fair share of ads as a teen on the bus and train heading to school or a friend's house. They came in all sizes and advertised everything from legal services and Broadway shows to job training programs and public safety announcements. Each one represented someone selling something—whether a product, service, or lifestyle. Some were hard to read, and most were easy to forget. That wasn't the case for a 2013 citywide public information campaign from Mayor Michael Bloomberg aimed at reducing teen pregnancy. The mayor and his administration posted bus and subway ads depicting distressed toddlers paired with slogans like, "Honestly, Mom, chances are he won't stay with you. What happens to me?" and "Dad, you'll be paying to support me for the next 20 years."[16] The campaign was immediately met with criticism for stigmatizing teen mothers, but the mayor's detractors were too consumed by anger to notice that one of the ads gave teens the three-step success sequence—"finish high school, get a job, and get married before having children"—to poverty-proof their lives.[17]

Regardless of what people feel about the execution, the ads showed that elected officials were willing to take a bold stance on an important issue related to family formation.

Mayor Bloomberg's controversial ad campaign was an example of how the bully pulpit can be used to influence public sentiment. Any municipal government in the country could follow New York City's example and direct city funding toward pro-marriage public awareness campaigns with simple messages like "Give her a ring before she gives you a baby" or "In this city we believe marriage comes before carriage." Some people will inevitably claim that these messages stigmatize parents who don't meet the ideals expressed in the ads, but I believe most neutral observers would see them as inspirational and aspirational. Elected officials and other government leaders can also use their platforms and influence to speak hard truths when necessary. No one would expect a mayor responding to a thirteen-year-old shooting suspect to ask "Where is this boy's father?" or state "I can't run the city and parent your children at the same time." Neither statement is directly tied to marriage, but both make it clear that a child's life outcomes depend far more on their home environment than a politician's policy agenda. These statements do not require any new laws or collaboration with another branch of government. All they require is an acknowledgement of the family's importance, an honest assessment of the government's limitations, courage, and political will.

The same ingredients are needed for other ideas that move beyond messaging campaigns. For instance, a marriage "boot camp" for cohabiting couples with children might be viewed with skepticism at first, but a visionary leader with the right political skills could sell it. The federal government has earmarked grant funds for marriage education programs in the past, including $35 million for one initiative called Helping Every Area of Relationships Thrive—Adults (HEART).[18] While funded with public dollars, the boot camp could be administered by local churches and cover important topics like communication, money management, blended families, fidelity, and conflict resolution. The program would culminate with a communal wedding for couples who successfully complete training and are ready to say "I do." In addition to being able to invite family and friends to celebrate their special day, the bride and groom would also be paired with a mentor couple who could walk alongside them through both the highs and lows of married life.

The most innovative aspect of this program, however, would be to add a monetary incentive for couples to get—and stay—married. For example, each couple that completes the program could choose either a $10,000 gift on their wedding day or a $20,000 loan that is fully forgiven after ten years. Either option would be paid through foundations or private donors, not government funds. There would be provisions to discourage bad actors and sham marriages, and much would depend on proper vetting and recruiting of program participants. The larger amount would be attractive to couples who are confident they will stay together and would discourage the idea of divorce during temporary periods of relationship turbulence.

It is very possible that this type of program would be met with resistance from both sides of the political aisle. Many conservatives who believe in the importance of marriage will be skeptical of the large financial incentive and state that "we can't throw money at problems" like rebuilding the family. Given the perverse incentives of welfare programs and general suspicion of big government, their cynicism is understandable. It's also shortsighted. Unlike other relationship education programs with vague qualitative metrics for determining success, the efficacy of a marriage boot camp would be assessed with more quantitative measures. To put it another way, it is far harder to claim that a program "works" when success is based on feelings about your relationship rather than on the number of couples saying "I do" on their wedding day.

Tangible and measurable goals are one strength of a program like this, but conservatives will also have to wrestle with a more fundamental reality. Working to cultivate marriage with low-income couples who come from single-parent homes and live in neighborhoods where intact families are rare is going to look different than the same work being done with college-educated, middle-class, churchgoing couples. To use a sports analogy, success must always be defined in the context of the game being played. This is why a baseball player with a .350 lifetime batting average could play for twenty years and walk into the MLB Hall of Fame, while a guard who shoots 35 percent from the free-throw line would have a very short NBA career.

The pushback from progressives—including many black Democrats—would sound a bit different. Government spending is typically not a problem for liberals, but a program that *promotes* traditional marriage certainly would be. My reference earlier in the book to the Washington, DC, program that gave $10,800 to low-income mothers is proof that progressive family strengthening initiatives are generally focused on the immediate needs of moms and their children, not the type of long-term community transformation that requires a culture of marriage to take root. Democrats will expend financial, political, and social capital on any issues they believe explain persistent racial disparities. These include education spending, income inequality, food insecurity, mass incarceration, housing instability, and gentrification. For some reason, family structure never makes the cut. A marriage boot camp for couples who already share a home and at least one child would address their economic needs and establish new norms for children whose default for male–female relationships and family dynamics is "baby mama" and "baby daddy," not husband and wife.

Government officials must be encouraged by any means necessary to use the tools at their disposal to proclaim the importance of marriage and the connection between family structure and social outcomes. This has traditionally been a bipartisan affair, but marriage promotion—whether through law or language—is coded as a "conservative" priority in today's political ecosystem. This is one reason rebuilding the black family will also require a transformation of black America's social and cultural priorities that puts politics in its proper place. Much of the left's policy agenda, from social welfare spending to abortion, depends on a weakened family structure. But at some point, black progressives need to ask themselves which would do more to uplift the race: 90 percent support for Democrats or 90 percent of black babies being born to married parents. The answer to that question should determine which relationship—marital or political—we prioritize moving forward.

Conclusion

One of the origins of the word *culture* is the Latin word *cultūra*, which is an agricultural term related to tilling land and the intentional preparation of the earth for fruitful activity. The principles that hold true in agriculture also apply to marriage culture, which is why institutions must be intentional about "planting" and "feeding" the values that strengthen families and "pruning" anything that weakens them. Rebuilding the black family will require major contributions from religious leaders, educators, and elected officials. There will also be a role for civil rights organizations and media outlets that cater to an African American audience. Churches running "spouse schools" for young couples, cities doing public awareness campaigns promoting family life, and scholars publishing best practices on strengthening marriage would all add to a revival movement. Some of these plans will be met with skepticism, both from elites across the political spectrum and from people in neighborhoods where a culture of marriage has not existed for decades. Couples in these "marriage deserts" can begin to change this dynamic by modeling love, respect, and mutual support, but institutions have the resources and influence to supercharge family revival.

Pastors committed to teaching biblical truth about sex, marriage, and family will do far more for the health and welfare of the black community than preachers who take their cues on family matters from the current page in the progressive political playbook. Likewise, civil rights and racial justice organizations today may ignore the decline in marriage in favor of the left's policy priorities, but that would change if every HBCU president signed a pledge affirming their commitment to rebuilding the black family and urged outside groups to follow suit. While the government must maintain its commitment to nondiscrimination, public awareness campaigns promoting a culture of marriage should reflect the populations they are meant to reach. Churches and nonprofits that use federal funding to run marriage education programs in cities like Washington, DC, Philadelphia, St. Louis, Jackson, Memphis, and Detroit will inevitably end up benefiting black families.

American institutions have played a role in undermining the family for decades, from the universities that have been a breeding ground for feminist activism since the 1960s to the public schools that engage students in discussions about sexual orientation and gender identity without parental consent.

Someone attending a progressive church is far more likely to see a Pride flag hanging outside than to hear a sermon from Genesis declaring that marriage is between one man and one woman. The destructive effect these institutions have had on the family is one reason shame needs to be consciously utilized as a tool for encouraging virtuous conduct and correcting bad behavior.

While the public criticism of politicians, pundits, professors, preachers, and performers will get the most attention, it would be a mistake to discount the power of proximity and positive affirmation when creating a culture of marriage. People must become more comfortable encouraging their loved ones to form strong families and correcting those who have a habit of making bad relationship choices. Some of these conversations will not be easy. Well-intentioned friends will be accused of being mean and judgmental. Outspoken elders may get the cold shoulder from the young people at family gatherings. But it is better for adults to hear words that make them uncomfortable—whether from the institutions that serve them or the people who love them—than for children to suffer the consequences of broken homes.

SEVEN

Remove Political Obstacles

From the founding of the group Black Lives Matter (BLM) in 2013 to its fall from grace in 2023 amid allegations of financial mismanagement, not a single journalist bothered to ask cofounders Alicia Garza and Patrisse Cullors an obvious question: Why would a movement fighting for racial uplift be committed to "disrupting" the nuclear family?

The two women helped start BLM after the acquittal of George Zimmerman in the killing of Trayvon Martin, and they gained international support in 2020 after video capturing George Floyd's final moments of life went viral across the world. Despite public health lockdowns brought on by COVID-19, millions of people across the country hit the streets to protest with BLM signs in hand. The cofounders were featured on the cover of *Time* magazine. The organization raised $90 million in donations in 2020 alone. Its eponymous slogan was painted on NBA courts and emblazoned on banners in NFL stadiums. The mayor of Washington, DC, Muriel Bowser, renamed a section of Sixteenth Street Northwest—walking distance from the White House—Black Lives Matter Plaza. Professional athletes, members of Congress, and corporate

CEOs knelt in solidarity with BLM protesters across the country in response to the racial reckoning sparked by Floyd's death. Universities put out statements supporting the organization. But no one seemed to care that the organization had declared war on the family.

I was familiar with BLM well before 2020 and had long wondered why an organization that claimed to oppose acts of police violence against black men never actually used the words "police" or "brutality" in any of its guiding principles. Oddly enough, BLM did discuss the traditional family, and it was these views that caught my attention, specifically the text of their "Black Villages" principle:

> We disrupt the Western-prescribed nuclear family structure requirement by supporting each other as extended families and "villages" that collectively care for one another, especially our children, to the degree that mothers, parents, and children are comfortable.[1]

That statement should have set off alarm bells among the politicians, journalists, preachers, and athletes promoting BLM as a movement for black liberation. I kept waiting for someone in progressive media to ask Garza and Cullors why their vision for the "village" didn't include any fathers and what made them believe too many *intact* families was a problem for the black community. Unfortunately, no one did. It likely never occurred to anyone to do so because BLM was just like every other racial justice organization in America, promising to fight "white supremacy" and "liberate" black people from the oppression of capitalism, racism, sexism, homophobia, and transphobia.

Black Lives Matter is the most influential movement claiming to fight for the rights of black people since the 1960s. The group's success in capturing the attention of the nation and convincing every institution to repeat its mantra concealed its radical anti-family worldview. And it's a worldview shared by the collection of ideologues and interest groups that came to make up the Black Lives Matter movement. This is why BLM matters for our purposes—not because this particular organization will be our primary opponent as we attempt to revive the family, but because it was the Black Lives Matter movement that collected and revealed a radical coalition of marriage mischief-makers who hid behind the rhetoric of racial justice while undermining black families. The members of this coalition will be the loudest opponents of our movement to rebuild the home.

They include:

1. *Feminists.* BLM's cofounders applied an intersectional feminist lens that uplifted black women and didn't mention "black men" even once when describing its core values. Likewise, feminist opponents of a revival movement will see an emphasis on traditional roles and marriage as a step back for women.

2. *Abortionists.* BLM was vocally pro-abortion and in the wake of the *Dobbs* decision stated, "As we continue our fight for freedom, we recognize that full access to abortion care is necessary for all Black people."[2] Abortionists understand that broken families feed their industry and have no incentive to support anything that will negatively impact their bottom line.

3. *LGBT Activists.* The LGBT bona fides of BLM have never been in doubt, evidenced by the fact Garza and Cullors

identify as "queer" and the organization's stated commitment to "dismantle cisgender privilege and uplift Black trans folk."[3] These ideologues think the traditional family structure is too restrictive and will prioritize LGBT inclusion over what's best for children.

4. *Functional Atheists.* As BLM showed, though the sexual politics of its cofounders were certainly out of step with biblical teaching, their stated devotion to "racial justice" was enough to convince many black pastors to endorse the movement. These people support the biblical blueprint for the family but don't want to impose their views on others.

5. *Antiracists.* BLM's commitment to fight "white supremacy" likely drew in supporters who would not support a civil rights movement led by black pastors. Antiracists think racial progress is tied more to ending white supremacy than rebuilding the black family.

6. *Paternalists.* Another view that made BLM popular in 2020 was the "defund the police" movement and the left's desire to slash funding for law enforcement and reallocate it to social welfare programs. Big-government liberals believe government programs—not intact families—are the key to positive social outcomes for single mothers and their children.

I call this collective that defined BLM and will fight our pro-family movement the Sinister Six, because although none would admit being driven by malicious intent, each one has contributed to the current state of the black family. What makes them particularly dangerous is their current involvement in the black cultural ecosystem, both through public policy and social norms.

This combination of bad ideas and cultural proximity explains why these groups are a political obstacle that must be removed for family revival to take root in black America. In many respects, the rules of agriculture also apply to the hard work of creating a marriage culture. Good values and behaviors must be planted and nourished, while self-destructive ideas and practices must be weeded and pruned. Defeating the Sinister Six requires understanding the arguments fueling their opposition as well as preparing for the criticism they will direct at a black marriage movement. The rest of this chapter will equip revivalists to do both.

Feminists

If feminists were honest revolutionaries, they would change their slogan from "Smash the Patriarchy" to "Mission Accomplished." The numbers don't lie. Single women in America own 2.72 million more homes than single men.[4] More women are primary breadwinners than ever before. Women earn close to 60 percent of bachelor's degrees today, compared with 35 percent in 1960.[5] The sex disparity in higher education is even more stark among African Americans, where black women today earn about 65 percent of bachelor's degrees and roughly 70 percent of master's degrees and PhDs.[6] Even social norms related to love and relationships have changed. Magazines like *Teen Vogue* write articles defending sex work but would never publish a modesty manifesto urging women to be more ladylike.

Second-wave feminists achieved their goals of convincing women that they are better off prioritizing a career over marriage and children. The development of black feminism as a distinct political ideology helps explain why every institution and industry concerned with racial equity focuses its efforts on black *women*, not men. One *USA Today* tweet made this point quite clear.

> After George Floyd's death, corporate America pledged to improve diversity in hiring. But two years later, deep racial inequities still exist when it comes to who gets the jobs with the most pay, perks and power—especially for Black women.[7]

While the gains black women have made in education, government, business, media, and politics garner positive attention, they have come at a cost. From 1890 through 1970, black women were more likely than white women to be married by thirty-five, and less than 10 percent were unwed by that age.[8] Today, 44 percent of black women between thirty-five and forty-four have never been married, compared with 16 percent of white women.[9]

No one should be surprised when the black feminists in academia, media, politics, and business *today* are the loudest critics of a family revival movement, especially one built on a biblical blueprint.

It is easy to caricature the inevitable pushback in radical, fist-in-the-air, "I don't need a man" terms. Yes, a subset of feminists will sound like Brittney Cooper and claim that intact families are not needed for the black community to thrive. The truth, however, is that pushback on a family revival movement will be far more likely to take the form of assertions that prioritizing a family will come at the cost of all the trappings of material success that black women have been told will bring personal fulfillment.

No one wants to be married to a person who makes their life more difficult, which is why feminists—many unmarried themselves—use scare tactics to brainwash the sisterhood. A woman who expresses a desire to be a stay-at-home mom will be told stories of a wife whose husband was controlling and unfaithful before leaving his family for a younger woman. The same person wouldn't tell a young woman who wants to go to college that she may get a degree in a dying industry and be saddled with debt. Likewise, they don't tell single, career-minded women they may wake up one day in a huge house and break out in tears because they have no husband and children who make it feel like *home.*

Some feminists will argue that an emphasis on marriage and family is just an attempt by black men to "put black women back in their place." To some extent, they are correct—as long as you understand that finding one's place isn't negative. One of the reasons that black women, including public figures, frequently talk about being burdened and carrying the weight of the world on their shoulders is because they have been filling a role that was not designed for them. It's hard enough to raise children with a present and involved husband, but that task is exponentially more difficult when you are the sole provider and caregiver. Life feels even heavier for the black women who see themselves as the "backbone" of their community and political party. This is more weight than women are built to bear.

There is a popular diagram that uses a multi-tiered umbrella to depict biblical order in the home.[10] It shows the children under the wife, the wife under the husband, and the husband under Christ. The image teaches a very important lesson about spiritual protection. A man who holds his umbrella over his wife and children as they walk through the rain is sending a clear signal that what is under his covering has more value to him than his own convenience. He is willing to be soaked if it means keeping his family dry because people protect what they value. A family revival movement is an attempt to reestablish peace and order in the home by having everyone play their God-given role.

While black feminists will be the most vocal critics, their white counterparts in the media will also have something to say. These women already use their platforms to criticize conservatives who promote marriage and family in the public square. In the words of one (married) writer at *New York* magazine:

> I have observed with dismay the building wave of solemn advice from social scientists, pundits, and politicians that the answer to the assorted ills of single American men and women (but especially women) is marriage.[11]

There is no reason to believe that anyone who thinks this way will be supportive of a black marriage movement, especially when liberal white women in the media have shown their willingness to attack conservative black men who reject progressive orthodoxy. I would respond to their pushback by asking what gives them the authority to dictate discourse around the black family.

In some respects, black family revival will require fighting a battle that is more than six decades in the making. Black feminists in the 1960s mimicked many of the arguments being made by the white women leading the mainstream movement, but the results for the two groups couldn't be any more different. A revivalist movement should not allow itself to be sidetracked by married white feminists in major publications writing op-eds that dismiss the importance of intact families before heading home to their husbands and children. That "do as I say, not as I do" approach to family formation is the hallmark of a self-serving ideologue, not a concerned ally.

A revival movement won't just be opposed by hypocritical women. There will also be male feminist foes arguing that "patriarchy," capitalism, and racism are the intersectional cords of oppression that keep black women bound. These men wear shirts that say "Listen to Black Women," and while many are married, they publicly express skepticism of male leadership. The response to them should be to inquire whether they feel any responsibility to protect and provide for their wives and children. If they answer in the affirmative, they should be forced to explain why they won't preach in public what they practice at home.

Feminists of every stripe speak as if marriage advocates believe that simply saying "I do" at the altar guarantees a perfect life. The truth is that life is difficult regardless of your relationship status. Marriage is no magic bullet for the challenges of life. Neither is a college degree, a C-suite job, or a well-earned frequent flyer status. But marriage is the most time-tested relational arrangement for lifelong romantic companionship and personal fulfillment while providing the foundation of the best family structure for raising children. It will be hard for even the most committed feminists to criticize the idea that children benefit from being raised in loving, two-parent homes. But for them, debates over marriage and family have never been about children. They are concerned only about the self-centered "needs" of "liberated" women. That's why the intensity of their opposition will ratchet up the moment a black marriage movement argues for the sanctity of life and the protection of all children, including those in the womb. Abortion has become such a staple of feminism that its most zealous advocates present a unique challenge to a black marriage movement—one that must be addressed directly.

Abortionists

The most destructive impact feminists have had on the black family since the 1960s has been convincing black women—and men—that aborting our offspring is an act of empowerment needed for African Americans to be truly "liberated" from oppression. Planned Parenthood and other abortion advocates hide their poison in euphemisms like "reproductive justice" or by claiming that "abortion is healthcare." What they don't tell the public is that 87 percent of women seeking abortions are unmarried, which suggest a mom-to-be is far less likely to end the life of her unborn child when the father is her husband.[12] The steep decline in African American marriage rates since the 1960s helps explain the heavy toll abortion has taken on the black family and is one reason black elites should be using their financial resources, political capital, and cultural influence to broadcast the benefits of putting marriage *before* the baby carriage. Such a significant shift in priorities would result in both stronger families *and* fewer abortions.

Abortionists' penchant for deceptive rhetoric will carry over into their strategy for opposing a movement to restore the black family. They will need to thread a narrative needle because it is much easier for abortionists to push back on white, male, pro-life legislators seeking to change abortion laws than on black Christians seeking to promote life by encouraging marriage. This is where Planned Parenthood will rely on its secret weapon: the Afristocracy. The organization's vice grip on the black community is revealed both by the babies it aborts and the leaders it supports. As I stated in an earlier chapter, the most influential black civil rights organizations, institutions, media outlets, elected officials, public intellectuals, and entertainers are pro-abortion. The NAACP, National

Urban League, Congressional Black Caucus, and BET all fight harder for abortion than for the black family.

Understanding how abortionists and their allies use racialized language to manipulate black voters is a critical part of inoculating the revival movement. Abortionists already claim that pro-life laws that decrease abortion are an attack on black women. This explains why, in the wake of the 2022 *Dobbs* decision, *PBS NewsHour* published an article titled "Black and Hispanic People Have the Most to Lose if *Roe* Is Overturned."[13] The same twisted logic explains why abortion is framed as a "racial justice" issue in progressive media.[14] Unabashedly pro-life revivalists will be accused of rolling back the clock on black women and turning them into "breeders" with no constitutional rights who are forced to give birth like their enslaved foremothers.

Using this type of reasoning, abortionists deserve the most contempt out of all the groups that constitute the Sinister Six. They hide their "deathcare" industry behind claims they are providing essential health services to poor black women. Yet any organization that declares that "black lives matter" one moment and argues that aborting black babies is a form of racial justice the next should be treated like a hostile enemy. Revivalists must refuse to make peace with institutions that are at war with our families.

One strategy for responding to them is to lean into the parallels *they* draw between abortion and slavery. For example, both chattel slavery and abortion deny the inherent dignity and worth of humans who are made in the image of God. Both view human beings as valuable only to the extent that they enrich the lives of their "owners," who argue that they alone have the right to choose the fate of their property. Both rely heavily on euphemism to hide the barbarity of each practice—"peculiar institution" in the case of slavery and the "right to choose" and "reproductive justice" in the case of abortion.

It is also important to note that if *conservatives* were the ones telling poor black women to abort their babies, the reaction from civil rights organizations and race commentators would likely be very different from the affirming stance they take today. The political left knows it can promote abortion if pro-life laws are framed as aiding and abetting "white supremacy." For some reason, the progressives who blame every disparity in social outcomes on racism become deaf, blind, and mute when it comes to abortion. Abortionists have done a masterful job at turning the survival of their industry into a racial justice issue, but one question to Planned Parenthood and the Afristocrats who support them would expose the idiocy of that argument in mere seconds: "Would a Klan member in the 1940s see fewer black babies being born due to abortion as a good or bad thing for society?"

It's easy to see why an organization started by a eugenicist would duplicitously target black women with their advertising and claim that abortion bans are rooted in white supremacy. I get why a political party that believes women have a human right to kill their offspring would make abortion one of its top policy priorities. The fact that radical feminists tend to be abortion absolutists makes sense logically. What is harder to understand is why *black* people support any cultural or policy agenda promoting the idea that a baby is better off being killed in the womb than born to a mother with too much melanin and not enough money. Some serious soul-searching needs to be done to figure out why *we* are so hell-bent on destroying our own children. About 40 percent of aborted babies in America are black.[15] In Georgia, 69 percent of aborted babies are black as are 80 percent in Mississippi.[16] Revivalists must be willing to fight *anyone* selling the idea that black women need to kill their babies to be truly liberated. We need to saturate the culture with the reality that children are a gift from God, not a burden that blocks a woman from a truly fulfilled life.

LGBT Activists

Legacy civil rights organizations have not only become vocal advocates for abortion. To borrow the language of the left, they have also been "colonized" by LGBT activists and spend far more time fighting for "trans rights" than for the black family. Their promotion of Pride politics is one reason black family revivalists should expect the opposition from LGBT activists to be loud and forceful. Groups like the Human Rights Campaign will argue that a biblical blueprint for marriage and a child-centric approach to family does not include the gender identities and sexual orientations that constitute the LGBT coalition. This is the sanitized and intellectual way to explain their opposition. In reality, they will treat anyone promoting traditional views on sex, sexuality, marriage, and family like an uninformed ally in need of re-education or a bigot in need of condemnation.

Malik Yoba is an actor who is most famous for playing the role of detective J. C. Williams in the 1990s police drama *New York Undercover.* It was his role in a gender identity struggle session, however, that foreshadows LGBT opposition to a biblically grounded black marriage movement. Yoba was a guest on *The Breakfast Club* radio show in 2019 alongside two self-identifying trans women and a man named David Johns, the executive director of the National Black Justice Coalition, a black LGBT civil rights organization.[17] At one point in the conversation Yoba used the phrase "naturally born woman" and was immediately corrected by Johns, who exclaimed, "nothing about that is natural" before instructing the actor to replace his appeal to biological sex with "for women who were assigned female at birth and for whom that is consistent with how they identify." Yoba stumbled a few times, but you could tell the actor was committed to learning his new lines.[18]

Malik Yoba was given a lecture for expressing biological reality, but he received grace from his activist comrades because they knew he was on their side. A black Christian like Tony Dungy, the Hall of Fame ex-NFL coach, should expect far more hostility for standing firm on his biblical views on marriage and family. Dungy is the first black head coach to win a Super Bowl and is respected for his professional accomplishments as well as his work off the field promoting faith, family, and fatherhood. But to progressive sportswriter Dave Zirin, Dungy is simply an "anti-gay bigot" who speaks at conferences organized by people who are "violently homophobic."[19] His sentiment is shared by *USA Today* columnist Nancy Armour, who has written that "Dungy, like so many others, has used his faith as justification for discriminating against LGBTQ people, claiming homosexuality is antithetical to his Christian beliefs."[20]

The responses to Tony Dungy are proof that LGBT criticism of Christian views on marriage and family are about beliefs, not tone. Dungy is the epitome of winsomeness, yet his gentle demeanor does not protect him from accusations of hatred. Likewise, anyone publicly promoting a black family revival movement should expect to be accused by pro-black activists of bigotry and upholding "white supremacy," no matter how politely they couch their language. Christians who refuse to pledge allegiance to the Pride flag also need to prepare themselves to be criticized by civil rights organizations that will compare them to cross-burning Klansmen in the Jim Crow South.

Responding to these personal attacks will require courage, clarity, conviction, and consistency. Black family advocates must rest assured that biology is not bigotry and be willing to say so publicly. Regardless of what identities they claim or how they feel, the fact remains that neither two men nor two women can make a baby. No one who rejects the laws of procreation has a "right" to a child they cannot—or did not—create. The only right involved in an effort to rebuild the traditional black family is the right every child has to be loved and protected by the man and woman who gave them life. This right is best exercised in a stable, loving home with their married biological parents. People who practice lifestyles that will never produce children naturally can't demand that a marriage and family movement cater to their needs. Bending to the criticism of LGBT activists would also be unwise from a purely statistical perspective. According to the Williams Institute, a public policy think tank at the UCLA School of Law, black LGBT adults raising children account for less than 1 percent of the total black population.[21] The US Census Bureau's 2022 report on American families and living arrangements found that married same-sex couples made up 0.5 percent of all black families.[22] Regardless of the rhetorical tactics they use, LGBT activists shouldn't be allowed to hijack a black marriage movement and force the demands of an infinitesimal percentage of adults to take priority over the family structure that is best for 100 percent of children.

Functional Atheists

Roughly three in four black adults identifies as a Christian, a higher percentage than any other racial group in the United States.[23] Even among Americans who are either atheist, agnostic, or of no particular faith, blacks are more likely (27 percent) than the overall population of religious "nones" (10 percent) to say that believing in God is needed to be a moral person.[24] To say that the church plays an important role in black life is an understatement. The church has been central to the education, moral instruction, social life, and political engagement of African Americans going back to the days of slavery.

However important the church has been as a cultural institution, many black Christians—including pastors—are functional atheists when it comes to family matters. Many of these individuals attend church regularly, are married, and love their families. They support the idea of "black love" and believe in the benefits of marriage. It is easy to assume they would be natural allies of a revival movement, but what makes them a political obstacle instead is their unwillingness to publicly endorse the belief that marriage is *necessary* for the purpose of starting a family. Their response to a black marriage movement will more likely be apathy than outright antagonism, largely because functional atheists are terrified of committing the "sin" of judgment. Many of them embody the marriage-before-carriage approach to family formation and teach their children to follow the same script. They simply refuse to preach what they practice out of concern they would be imposing their views on anyone else.

The disconnect between observed behaviors and expressed values is one consequence of the black church's preoccupation with politics. The irony is that one Pew research study found that black Protestants are more than three times as likely to say that one of a church's essential roles is to "offer moral guidance" (73 percent) than preach sermons addressing political topics (24 percent).[25] Unfortunately, many of the most influential black churches seem to take the opposite view.

Their focus on politics has contributed to the loss of the theological grounding needed to help either their congregants or the larger community think biblically about sex, sexuality, marriage, and family. In fact, it's often black pastors who are leading the flock away from biblical truth. As I wrote in an earlier chapter, Senator Raphael Warnock's dual vocations as both a federal legislator and pastor epitomize the black church archetype: socially conscious, politically active, civically engaged, and spiritually dead. Warnock's abandonment of biblical teaching on marriage and family is not disqualifying, because for many functional atheists, getting "souls to the polls" on Election Day is a greater sign of institutional health for black churches than is preaching about the spiritual significance and social benefits of marriage.

The best way to respond to functional atheists is to appeal to their stated profession of Christian faith. Anyone who says they love God should be prepared to explain why they disregard biblical teaching on marriage and family or ignore the topic altogether. The fear many functional atheists have of being judgmental must also be addressed. One way to do this is by acknowledging that public opinion—in addition to biblical morality—is on their side. While black children are far more likely than children of any other race to live with a single mother, one Pew survey found that 46 percent of African Americans believed that single women raising children on their own is bad for society.[26] While most black respondents said single motherhood was either good (9 percent) or doesn't make a difference (45 percent), the fact that 50 percent of black children are raised by a single parent means the data suggest a significant number of people are willing to criticize their own behavior or that of someone they know.[27] That may sound counterintuitive, but in my experience, struggling single mothers are more honest about the challenges of raising children without a father than the elites who practice the marriage-before-carriage approach to forming a family but use their platforms and influence to defend baby mama culture.

The same phenomenon exists in other areas. For instance, the percentage of blacks and whites who have ever cohabited is roughly the same—59 percent and 62 percent, respectively—but African Americans are less accepting of cohabitation than their white and Hispanic counterparts.[28] In a perfect world, black Christians would speak the truth even if public opinion is not on their side, but these figures give some hope that functional atheists are a sleeping giant that can eventually be awakened from their spiritual slumber.

Antiracists

Though they are not a religious group, idolatry drives the antiracists who believe defeating "white supremacy" is a more worthy investment of political, economic, and cultural capital than rebuilding the black family. Their worldview is powered by a perverse twisting of scripture. They think "black people shall not live on bread alone, but on every word that comes from the mouths of white people." Led by people like Ibram X. Kendi, they talk a good game about empowerment while promoting the idea that the actions of white people are what ultimately determine outcomes for black people.

Their opposition to a renewed focus on the black family will be equally motivated by ideology and self-interest. Antiracists use the plight of working-class blacks to blackmail wealthy liberal whites. Their entire business model is based on the "reverse Robin Hood" mindset applied to race politics. They steal valuable currency— narratives, experiences, and outcomes—from the poor to extract benefits for themselves. Several outlets noted that Kendi saw renewed interest in his book *How to Be an Antiracist* after the death of George Floyd. He also launched his Center for Antiracist Research at Boston University in 2020, and it raked in more than $40 million over three years before facing public allegations of financial mismanagement.[29] Other Kendi clones have proven equally successful at turning antiracism into an industry. They do everything from hosting conferences to pushing curricula in K–12 schools and corporate settings.

One *USA Today* article entitled "Anti-Racist Book Dethrones 'Hunger Games' Prequel on Best-Seller List amid Mass Protests" mentioned Kendi's book as well as Robin DiAngelo's *White Fragility*, the manifesto for guilty white liberals.[30] With DiAngelo, we see that it's not just money but a feeling of superiority that fuels the antiracism industry. DiAngelo and her followers will dismiss a revival movement because talking about marriage and family structure does not help them live out their savior complex. DiAngelo prefers blacks who, like her, believe that being white is a "privilege," a worldview that ends up treating melanated skin like a congenital defect. These white antiracists carry shame about America's complicated racial history and would hate to lose their status—and jobs— as "good white people" willing to use their social capital to "help" black people. The beauty of a revival movement is that it has no use for white liberal self-righteous self-flagellation. DiAngelo and her acolytes will have a hard time with a revival movement because it's hard to hear "I don't need you" from the people you've been told depend on you for improving the quality of their lives.

Whether driven by money or self-importance, both groups of antiracists will have no interest in a revival movement, because whether a black man decides to marry a black woman before having a child with her is not something that can be blamed on white people. Antiracists are deeply invested in addressing every racial disparity except anything that involves family structure. We can see it everywhere. The local government in Washington, DC, published a racial equity plan that included several indicators that would be used to quantify disparities between blacks and whites in the nation's capital. The plan included outcome measures related to K–12 education, unemployment, and obesity. But the city also wanted to track the percent of spaces owned by city government that are named for "BIPOC" (Black, Indigenous, and People of Color) individuals.[31] The number of references to marriage or family structure? You guessed it: zero.

Our response to antiracists needs to be clear and straightforward. Revivalists must reject the toxic combination of white guilt and black self-debasement that powers their industry and expose it at every turn. They should be asked why the black family was more intact at a time when anti-black racism was baked into American law and social custom than it is today. They should be forced to answer how black civil rights lawyers went from fighting segregation in the Jim Crow era to celebrating the elimination of "master bedroom" from real estate listings in 2021.[32] Activists and civil rights organizations should be asked to explain how getting white people to read books, attend conferences, watch documentaries, or support causes tied to antiracism will benefit the black community more than a renewed commitment to building stronger families. Ultimately, they must be challenged with the truth that success starts at home, not with self-serving race merchants who think that uplift can be outsourced.

Paternalists

The last group of revival obstructionists will be the politicians, pundits, cultural commentators, and activists who believe focusing on the family is a distraction from the types of government programs that could bring about systemic change and racial justice. Their way of thinking has dominated public policy and political discourse since the 1960s, and the pushback from this group will take two separate but related forms.

Macro-paternalists will argue that electing more Democrats at every level of government—especially federal—will improve social outcomes and bring about racial uplift. Their focus will largely be on electing black candidates, especially women, to national office. They will also celebrate the black mayors running America's largest cities as a win for black people more generally. Their version of paternalism casts Democrats as protectors who will take care of black voters once in office. The second group of paternalists operates on a micro level and sees government—especially local— as the primary provider for black women and their children. To them, the appropriate response to black family breakdown from elected officials and the unelected bureaucrats who run schools, police departments, and child welfare agencies is more funding for government programs. Many of these paternalists are sympathetic to the idea that family structure is connected to the social ills that plague our largest cities. They just don't believe that a marriage movement is practical, and, like their counterparts at the federal level, they do not want to do anything to alienate their voters and constituents.

Both groups of paternalists will make the same types of arguments. They will say that the government doesn't have the tools and resources to rebuild the family. They will also claim that it is impractical to preach the necessity of marriage in communities where weddings rarely precede the birth of a baby and most children live with a single mother. Though rarely stated explicitly, the crux of the paternalist argument is that marriage and intact families are not necessary if mothers and children have access to government programs and services.

Macro-paternalists will argue that talking about the black family is a distraction from the real issues causing racial inequities. They would prefer to focus on raising taxes on the rich, increasing the minimum wage, and fighting for affordable housing, healthcare, criminal justice reform, and voting rights. Their priorities always translate into calls for people to "get out and vote" if they want to see change in their communities. Micro-paternalists will say that what black families in the inner city really need are fully funded and integrated schools, recreation centers with youth programs and extended hours, libraries with the latest books and computers, new parks and athletic fields, and employment programs. One of the defining features of paternalist thinking is the complete absence of the family in any of the plans to improve outcomes. They seem to think that politicians and government administrators have more influence on the trajectory of a little black girl's life than the man and women that created her. Paternalists look at racial disparities in both the schoolhouse and jailhouse and assume the government must fix the problem.

An important feature of the paternalist opposition will be its distinct racial dynamic. Black Democrats who work in local government or nonprofits that provide services in low-income neighborhoods will likely be far more open to a marriage movement than the young white "tax the rich" progressives who are a key constituency in every big city and fill the ranks of left-leaning media outlets. Not only do these white paternalists think pushing for more government programs is preferable to focusing on the family, but they—like their feminist counterparts—also believe they know what's best for the black community.

Another trait many paternalists of every stripe share with feminists is their personal commitment to a marriage-before-carriage approach to family formation despite their public dismissal of marriage. This hypocrisy can lead us to ask them to explain their penchant for talking "left" but living "right." Some will respond that focusing on family structure is just a conservative exercise in "blaming the victim," but they should be asked whether they—personally—believe that *their* elected officials are responsible for the well-being of their children. Anyone who speaks and acts as if agency is for only white or wealthy people should be forced to say so publicly. Ultimately, paternalists need to be told that the racial uplift they desire will never materialize as long as the government remains the most important institution in the black community. They must accept the reality that family reconstruction will not occur on their preferred timeline of election cycles and that their opposition will ensure that whoever fills their seat forty years from now will be facing the same issues. Eventually, their constituents may start asking if that is their goal.

Conclusion

If the people opposing a movement to rebuild the black family were proud racists and bigots, there is no doubt that black leaders would respond with resistance. But since the Sinister Six all present themselves as angels of light, their darkened thinking will be welcomed by many "pro-black" commentators and treated as legitimate. If revivalists launched, for example, a "Black *Wives* Matter" campaign that promoted the necessity of marriage and goodness of family life, the loudest critics would be the groups I describe above. The idea that self-professed allies of the black community would be some of the biggest obstacles to a Black Wives Matter campaign is hard to accept for people whose cultural operating systems have not been updated since the 1960s. Even today, the standard narrative on race in all our most important institutions is that Republicans and white conservatives are enemies of black uplift, while Democrats and the multi-racial coalition of progressives are our friends.

But each group within the Sinister Six cares more about their ideological commitments than fighting for what's best for black families. In fact, part of what makes this coalition so powerful is the interconnectedness of each group. The cofounders of BLM showed that it was possible to combine several different progressive priorities into a single organization. This united force wrapped its pro-abortion, LGBT, feminist activism in a thin veil of pro-black antiracism so effectively that black churches and politicians ended up promoting self-professed Marxists.[33]

Resistance to a revival movement will be driven not only by the ideology of the Sinister Six but by identity as well. White feminists will write anti-marriage screeds at mainstream publications that dismiss black family breakdown before going home to their husbands. White liberals who have all their children within marriage will attempt to lecture revivalists about why black families need more government programs to get ahead. Civil rights organizations will dismiss the black families that will benefit from a renewed commitment to marriage in order to appease the mostly white LGBT community and Pride activists who believe that a biblical blueprint for rebuilding the home is bigoted and hateful. The recurring theme in each of these scenarios is clear: Black Democrats today are more invested in promoting the political priorities of white progressives than in rebuilding the black family. The divided loyalties of the Afristocracy will likewise complicate a family revival movement, but their misplaced allegiances won't be enough to impede progress if enough everyday people get on board. In some respects, a revival of marriage will serve as a revolt against the black leadership class and its worship of political idols.

The Sinister Six will be a major obstacle to a thriving family culture. Their arguments and influence must be countered and removed. But politics isn't the only obstacle to revival. There are also cultural impediments that must be addressed for a marriage movement to reach its full potential.

EIGHT

Reject Destructive Media

The late C. Delores Tucker was one of the most important black leaders of the twentieth century. The Philadelphia native participated in the civil rights movement in the 1960s, served as Secretary of the Commonwealth of Pennsylvania in the 1970s, and helped found the National Political Congress of Black Women in the 1980s. Tucker's accomplishments were impressive in their own right, but her status as a prophetic culture warrior was cemented in the 1990s when she went on a crusade against gangsta rap.

The National Rainbow Coalition, led by Rev. Jesse Jackson, held a meeting in Washington, DC, on January 6, 1994, to address violence against women in media and society. The event featured prominent black elected officials and scholars. Attorney General Janet Reno was also in attendance. But it was Tucker, seated next to Betty Shabazz, the widow of Malcolm X, who stole the show. Her prepared remarks were critical of the rappers she believed were poisoning their communities with lyrics that degraded women. She also excoriated the music executives who promoted artists who portrayed black women as the hypersexual playthings of hypermasculine rappers. She made her agenda clear when she declared,

"I am here to put the nation on notice that violence perpetuated against women through the music industry in the forms of gangster rap and misogynist lyrics will not be tolerated any longer."[1] Tucker specifically pointed to the release of Snoop Doggy Dogg's debut album *Doggystyle* and called its cover artwork "pornographic smut."[2] She was even critical of people who used the First Amendment to defend rappers who referred to women as "hoes," "bitches," and "sluts" in their songs.[3] Tucker's response to those people was clear: "No one has the right to degrade, denigrate, dishonor, or disrespect African-American women."[4] She closed her remarks by stating that she and her supporters were willing to go to jail to fight against the "social and psychological genocide" against the women and girls of the nation.[5] Young hip-hop fans in the 1990s largely sided with the artists Tucker criticized, especially after Tupac Shakur criticized her by name in his hit song "How Do U Want It." Shakur's label, Death Row, also pushed back on her activism with a civil lawsuit that suggested she had a financial motive for criticizing rappers.[6] The company's CEO, Suge Knight, claimed Tucker was a "phony" who was "pretending" to be a moral leader.[7] Other artists would criticize her efforts years later, including Eminem, who once rapped, "Tell that C. Delores Tucker slut to s*ck a d*ck."[8]

C. Delores Tucker was wise to sound the alarm about "continuously exposing our youth to negative media that distorts their images of male–female relationships, that undermines the stability of our families, communities, and nation by encouraging violence, abuse, and sexism as acceptable behaviors, and perpetuates the cycle of low self-esteem of African-American youth."[9] And like many prophets, she was rejected by the people she was trying to reach, who suffered the consequences of their rebellion. The comments under any YouTube video featuring old clips of Tucker always include replies from people who say they sided with Tupac and the other rappers at the time who disliked her crusade against them, but now, as adults, realize how right she was to speak out against the rappers pushing destructive lyrics. The commenters finally see what she knew back in the early 1990s: When it comes to the relationships between black men and black women that determine the health and strength of the black family, it is impossible to sow *Doggystyle* and reap the Huxtables.

Whatever anyone might think about Bill Cosby's personal failings after multiple women accused him of sexual assault, his careful construction of *The Cosby Show* and his lead character Cliff Huxtable was a testament to his belief that media can be used as a force for good. He brought in Harvard psychiatrist Dr. Alvin Poussaint as a consultant for the hit sitcom. Both men wanted the show to include positive images of a black family, including a loving relationship between Cliff and Clair Huxtable, the show's fictional husband and wife.[10] Cosby and Poussaint also wanted the show to exist in a black cultural context, evidenced by the African artwork, jazz, and references to historically black colleges that were a staple in the family's home.[11] The two men, like C. Delores Tucker, knew that music, television, and film were powerful tools for shaping how people see themselves, others, and the world around them. To them, the value of entertainment extended far beyond making money. Media was also a vehicle for the careful curation and cultivation of the black public image. That lesson still holds today. A movement to revive the family will never reach its full potential if black cultural capital is used to promote images of division, dysfunction, degeneracy, and destruction. Harnessing the power of media will require honest conversations about what, if any, responsibility black artists and entertainers have for the real-world impact of the content they create. It will also require honest self-reflection on the part of black consumers about the decision to support artists who produce content and promote values that sow seeds of self-hate, not "black love."

An Old Fight

When it comes to race in America during the twentieth century, many people instinctively think about the young men and women who risked their lives during the Civil Rights movement to end segregation and secure equal rights for black Americans. We think about Bloody Sunday and the Edmund Pettus Bridge, the Montgomery bus boycotts, and the 16th Street Baptist Church bombing. We also recognize key figures from that era, from Dr. Martin Luther King Jr. and Rosa Parks to George Wallace and Bull Connor.

One issue that does not get nearly as much attention is the battle that black leaders in previous generations waged to defend and preserve the image of African Americans in popular culture. They fought hard against racial stereotypes that painted black people as violent, hypersexual, immoral, lazy, unintelligent, and subservient. Tom Burrell is a pioneering advertising executive whose book *Brainwashed* details how media has been used to promote the idea of black inferiority throughout American history.

His book includes images of several of these stereotypes to drive home the point. At various points in American history, black people have been portrayed as the subservient "Uncle Tom," the rebellious "buck," the nurturing "mammy," the sexually promiscuous "Jezebel," and the argumentative "Sapphire." Depictions of "Negroes" in the nineteenth and twentieth centuries often included exaggerations of physical features, including skin color, lips, and eyes. The connection between phenotype and character traits was meant to send a clear signal that *black* was synonymous with *inferior*.

Black leaders in previous generations understood the power media and entertainment have in shaping perception. The film *The Birth of a Nation* was released in 1915 and earned praise for its filmmaking technique and cinematography.[12] President Woodrow Wilson hosted a screening for the film at the White House. But D. W. Griffith's Civil War epic also was criticized for its heroic portrayal of the Ku Klux Klan as well as depictions of black men—played by white actors in blackface—preying on white women. The NAACP, still a relatively young organization, was unsuccessful in getting the film pulled from theaters across the country.[13] But protests were not the only form of resistance to racial propaganda. Black directors and film companies used media to paint a different picture of race in America.

The Lincoln Motion Picture Company released *The Realization of a Negro's Ambition* in 1916.[14] The silent film is now lost, but its portrayal of a black man as an oil engineer was in stark contrast to typical images of African Americans at the time.[15]

Oscar Micheaux was the first major black filmmaker, directing more than forty films with predominantly black casts. His 1920 film *Within Our Gates* included middle-class black characters and is seen as a direct rebuttal to the racist portrayal of blacks in *The Birth of a Nation*.[16] Black leaders opposed racist propaganda because it infused dehumanizing stereotypes into the cultural bloodstream. These depictions shaped how white Americans saw their fellow citizens, but more importantly, they impacted how black Americans saw *themselves*. To this day, black professors, pundits, and cultural critics regularly refer to the negative impact *The Birth of a Nation* had on American culture, including the role it played in the resurgence of the Ku Klux Klan.[17] Yet somehow, the idea that mass media shapes our worldview is rejected when *black* artists, producers, and directors are the people propagating stereotypes.

"We Don't Love Them Hoes"

Rap music has been a mainstay in American culture for more than forty years. Hip-hop has influenced everything from fashion to slang and been enjoyed by everyone from latchkey kids in Harlem to teens in leafy suburbs. Rap's broad appeal does not mean it has had the same impact on all fans. Anyone who believes "kids want to be what they see" must apply that principle to hip-hop the same way they would law and medicine. There is some merit to the left's argument that black kids can be inspired to pursue certain activities and careers if they see black people in those roles. What black boys saw in the early 1990s was a steady stream of young men who looked like them glorifying violence and degrading women. The general perspective rappers had on the women in their orbit was summed up in the immortal words of Snoop Dogg: "We don't love them hoes."

Despite the criticism he received from C. Delores Tucker, Snoop, whose real name is Calvin Broadus Jr., went on to become an international superstar. The rapper and actor is now one of hip-hop's elder statesmen. He has been married to his wife since 1997 and has several grandchildren. But over the course of his career he has been open about his affiliation with the Crips street gang, bragged about being a pimp, and showed up to the 2003 MTV Video Music Awards with two scantily clad women on dog leashes.[18]

It would have been nice if Snoop had chosen to promote a family-man persona as he got older, but treating women like objects useful only for sexual pleasure has been a feature—not a bug—of commercial hip-hop for decades. The sexually explicit lyrics from the Miami-based hip-hop group 2 Live Crew were highly controversial in the 1980s. The cover art for their 1989 album *As Nasty as They Wanna Be* featured four women wearing bikinis and their nearly bare bottoms. Sheriff Nick Navarro of Broward County, Florida attempted to prevent record store owners from selling the album, and it was declared obscene by a federal district court.[19] That ruling was later overturned on appeal by the Eleventh Circuit in 1992.

It is much easier to name the handful of "conscious" and alternative hip-hop artists and groups than go down the list of rappers who promote negative images of black women. Groups from the early 1990s like The Fugees, A Tribe Called Quest, and De La Soul achieved commercial success but eventually gave way to the more hardcore artists who eventually came to dominate the hip-hop scene. The depictions of women in the two subgenres were quite different. Dr. Dre's song "Nuthin' but a 'G' Thang" is considered a classic by hip-hop fans and reached number two on the Billboard Hot 100 list in 1993.[20] The video features a baby-faced Snoop Dogg being picked up by Dr. Dre and heading to a block party. One scene shows a man pulling down the bikini top of a woman playing volleyball, exposing her breasts to the crowd. One of the final shots shows a woman—portrayed as stuck up and standoffish in the video—at a house party being doused with malt liquor.

Those interactions stand in stark contrast to the imagery promoted by Arrested Development, an Afrocentric, socially conscious rap group out of Atlanta. Their popular anthem "People Everyday" is about a man whose "black queen" was groped and disrespected by a group of drunk, belligerent men in a park.[21] Speech, the rap group's frontman, describes the encounter in a first-person narrative that includes his willingness to fight the men to defend his woman's honor. The song peaked at number eight on the Billboard Hot 100 in 1992 but has not had nearly the cultural impact as the collaboration between Dr. Dre and Snoop Dogg.[22]

The two songs don't just represent different points on the hip-hop spectrum. They also offer distinct archetypes for the relationship between the sexes within rap culture. Speech defended his woman and was willing to die for her. The men in Dr. Dre's video degraded and disrespected the women in their orbit. It is impossible to predict how rap would have developed as a genre if its more conscious subgenres dwarfed the more destructive ones in popularity. Ultimately, the influence of gangsta rap worried elders like C. Delores Tucker enough to raise concerns about the lyrics and imagery that saturated black culture in the 1990s.[23] They argued that music glorifying violence and degrading women would have a corrosive effect on the people who identified most closely with the artists. Their concerns were dismissed by people who prioritized the wealth of a few black artists over the cultural health of the broader community. Respected figures like Oprah Winfrey and Maya Angelou were also troubled by the messages being beamed out from rappers to black children. They opposed the artists infusing art with gratuitous violence, degrading sex acts, and enthusiastic drug use because they understood that the laws of sowing and reaping apply as much to pop culture as they do to agriculture. They knew black boys who watched St. Louis rapper Nelly's "Tip Drill" video and saw him slide a credit card down the backside of a woman probably wouldn't view her—or young ladies who looked like her—with much respect. They were ahead of their time. Unfortunately, their warnings were ignored and their motives attacked by the young men they criticized.

The siren song of street life, popularized and glamorized in hip-hop culture, exerts a gravitational pull on black boys across the country, whether they grow up poor in a big city or middle class in the suburbs. It makes boys who were raised like Cosby kids mimic the style, language, mannerisms, and behavior of gang members. A common response to this observation is that hip-hop record sales are driven by white consumers. I've heard this claim for years, and even if it is true, it is largely irrelevant. For young white men in the suburbs, rappers are tour guides narrating the perils of street life. White teens who try to mimic the speech patterns, behaviors, and fashion choices of their favorite artists are derided for "acting black." But for young black men, regardless of where they grow up or how they are raised, hip-hop is a culture that fits like a bespoke suit. No rapper or athlete in America has ever had his racial authenticity questioned for talking about his gang ties, drug sales, or sexual exploits. Yet for all the criticism that rap has received for its portrayals and treatment of women, the ascendance of female rappers has done little to turn down the sexualized nature of the genre.

No Shame in the Game

The 1993 song "U.N.I.T.Y." by Queen Latifah includes a memorable chorus and the line, "Who you callin' a bitch?!" as a direct response to the disrespect women in hip-hop had become accustomed to receiving.[24] Much like Roxanne Shanté and MC Lyte, Queen Latifah didn't use sex to sell records. The female artists who were pioneers in the genre wanted to be known as lyricists who could compete with the men. This is one reason that in the early 1990s, a semi-nude woman in a rap video was far more likely to be a "video vixen" than an emcee. That changed with the commercial success of artists like Lil' Kim and Foxy Brown later in the decade. Each made her sexuality a major part of her artistic brand. This was to the delight of sex-positive feminists but the detriment of future generations.

The commercial success of female artists like Nicki Minaj, Cardi B, and Megan Thee Stallion is built on a foundation laid by the female artists selling sex appeal who came before them. Their fame also shows how successful they have been at grabbing the flesh-peddling baton from their male counterparts and moving women in hip-hop from background eye candy to barely clothed main attraction. The message from the men who pioneered gangsta rap in the 1990s and the women who dominate hip-hop today is the same: Being degraded by people higher up on the social hierarchy is oppressive, but demeaning yourself and destroying the public image of your community for money and fame is empowering. Matriarchs of a previous generation, largely shaped by the black church, would have nipped that lie in the bud. They would have told the young women coming after them that they have more to offer the world than sex and assured them that no amount of success is worth their soul.

Today, rappers like Minaj—a married mother—give their stamp of approval to younger artists who have been shaped in their image. This is a two-way street of cultural self-destruction: The up-and-coming artist receives needed validation from an established veteran, while the aging star gets to ride the coattails of the hot newbie. This strategy is one of the main ways that cultural degeneracy spreads. The VH1 show *Love & Hip Hop* introduced most people to Cardi B. She teamed with Megan Thee Stallion to release the song "WAP," which won awards for song of the year from both BET and NPR. Cardi introduced many people to Sukihana, who appeared in the "WAP" music video and talked about being a "hoe" in a roundtable on Apple Music.[25] Sukihana is the person who helped platform Sexyy Red, whose song "Pound Town" included an anatomical acknowledgement that would have filled C. Delores Tucker with disgust.

I'm outta town, thuggin' with my rounds
My coochie pink, my booty-hole brown[26]

As repulsed as I am to write these lyrics, it is important for readers to know how accepted this type of filth has become and how little serious scrutiny it receives from the gatekeepers of black culture. Part of the reason is because a lot of people make money from it. The other is because black men in media and entertainment are terrified of being called sexist, misogynist, and hypocritical for speaking out on an issue *they* helped create.

A healthy culture would use its collective social capital and moral authority to shame someone like Sexyy Red into a different career choice. Cultural physicians would see her popularity as a sign that, metaphorically speaking, the malignant tumor of degradation and self-destruction that previous generations tried to fight had metastasized and spread to other parts of the body. Women rapping about their private parts still sell the same lie that an "alpha" female thinks, speaks, and behaves like a man. It communicates to young women that promiscuity is a good thing when *you* are in the driver's seat.

What the people pushing this ideology don't understand is that a woman who sees herself primarily as a sex object will never build a loving marriage for the same reasons as her sex-crazed male counterparts. Both prioritize temporary sexual fulfillment over long-term relationship commitment. Both treat the opposite sex as competition to be conquered, not companions to be cherished. Both prioritize sexual variety over stability in ways that become a breeding ground for infidelity and distrust. This is how you create a culture where children are plentiful but marriages are rare. Rap music didn't create these distorted relationship dynamics, but it has been their theme music for the better part of thirty years.

Image Is Everything

The downward spiral of hip-hop culture can be discouraging at times, especially to older artists and fans who express concerns about the values being promoted by younger acts. Thankfully, recent history has proven that an organized force of concerned black consumers can bring a powerful cadre of cultural contaminators to heel. The reality show *Sorority Sisters* premiered on VH1 December 15, 2014, to an audience of more than one million people. The show followed nine women from four historically black sororities: Alpha Kappa Alpha, Delta Sigma Theta, Zeta Phi Beta, and Sigma Gamma Rho. The trailer and first episode looked more like a *Love & Hip Hop* spinoff than a celebration of the black Greek-letter organizations that are well known today for their community service and have historically been incubators for the black leadership class since the early 1900s. Despite good initial ratings, *Sorority Sisters* was quickly pulled off the air. The reason why is a powerful case study in image management.

In the span of a few weeks, prominent members of black fraternities and sororities started a campaign and hashtag to get the show canceled.[27] Roland Martin, a member of Alpha Phi Alpha, appeared on *Morning Joe* and said the show denigrated black women.[28] Ava DuVernay, a member of Alpha Kappa Alpha, asked that commercials for her film *Selma* be pulled while the show aired.

Even K. Michelle, an R&B singer and Delta who built a following as a cast member of *Love & Hip Hop,* criticized the show publicly.[29] Sponsors got the message. Victoria's Secret, McDonald's, Sports Authority, Hallmark, Honda, Ford, State Farm, Crayola, Carmex, and even the NBA all pulled their ads from airing during the show.[30] VH1 responded to the pressure campaign and canceled the show one month after it premiered.

That was not the end of the story. Several women were kicked out of their sororities for being on the show, and one woman appeared on Steve Harvey's show to beg for forgiveness from one of her sorors (i.e., fellow sorority sisters).[31] Harvey, himself a member of Omega Psi Phi, explained the lifelong nature and cultural significance of black fraternities and sororities.

The black Greek community completely destroyed *Sorority Sisters.* They also demonstrated what organizations and institutions that value dignity, legacy, and community do when members forget who they are and what they are supposed to represent. Unfortunately, black professors, culture critics, journalists, and entertainers have made one excuse after another for decades in attempts to defend the violent, debauched, degrading, and self-destructive images that have become the norm within hip-hop culture. They have claimed that artists are simply acting as the "CNN of the hood" or reflecting the problems in society. But when it came to *Sorority Sisters,* in the span of a few weeks the black leadership class flexed its muscle and showed what it can do to protect the institutions it actually cares about. Public efforts to police behavior are typically derided as "respectability politics" by the Afristocracy, but the quick death of *Sorority Sisters* is proof that there are some lines people are unwilling to cross.

Good farmers both plant and prune. Likewise, wise leaders cultivate positive habits, reward hard work, and encourage members to think beyond themselves. They also remove negative influences by leveraging shame to promote conformity to group norms. The people who raised a collective ruckus to get VH1 to pull *Sorority Sisters* showed what effective "pruning" looks like in the public square. The same principles can be applied to the negative imagery permeating hip-hop culture, especially since other groups have provided a template.

In 2021, the rapper DaBaby made controversial comments at a concert about people with HIV and men engaged in sexual acts with other men. His entire rant lasted less than thirty seconds, but that was all the time needed to set off a wave of criticism from fans, fellow artists, and members of the LGBT community. The music industry heard the backlash loud and clear. DaBaby was dropped from at least seven music festivals following his comments.[32] He issued an apology on Instagram and received invitations from multiple organizations to educate him about HIV. The incident proved that even the most profane rappers can quickly find their manners with enough pressure from the right people. A Christian rapper named Bizzle captured the power dynamics within hip-hop perfectly in his song "Poppin":

Sad thing is how fast you could diss a Black queen
And turn around and walk on eggshells for a drag queen[33]

21 Savage is another artist who has a selective conscience. He frequently raps about guns and violence, without any sense that his words carry weight among young black men engaged in street life. But when LeBron James tweeted a lyric from his song "ASMR," both the rapper and NBA superstar made public apologies. The line in question?

We been getting that Jewish money, everything is kosher.[34]

The rapper later clarified that his lyric was a compliment to the business acumen and financial savvy of the Jewish people he knows personally.[35] Regardless of what people feel about this line, the fact that a rapper felt more remorse for it than songs about killing black men proves that artists will respond to social and financial pressure—but only when it is concentrated and consistent.

Revivalists should learn from the groups that make rappers weak-kneed and be willing to challenge the artists and record executives who push content that promotes strife between the sexes. This could take the form of boycotts, open letters, or social media pressure targeted at content creators or distributors. Ultimately, a drastic reduction in the demand for toxic content will eventually choke out its supply. Simply choosing not to consume music, movies, television, or any other content that features black faces promoting dysfunction is the most dignified way to remove destructive media from the culture.

Black consumers must not only voice disapproval for destructive and degrading content, but also demand, promote, create, and support the positive alternatives. Much like efforts to restore a marriage and family culture, one way to revive the positive contributions of black artists is to draw lessons from the past. The R&B group Jodeci had a sense of style that was closer to their contemporaries in hip-hop than the clean-cut look of their counterparts in Boyz II Men. That said, their song "Forever My Lady" was a popular ballad released in 1991 from the group's debut album. It starts with five words—"So you're having my baby"—and is sung from the perspective of a man who looks forward to starting a family with the mother of his child.

The song's declaration that "there's nothing more precious than to raise a family" stands in stark contrast to the pop artists today who push sex in their lyrics and promote abortion with their activism. The group SWV was similar to Jodeci in their seamless fusion of smooth vocals and hip-hop style. The three women from New York City sported long nails and dressed in everything from leather shorts to military fatigues. But much like their male counterparts, these artists wrote some of their most popular songs—including hits like "Weak" and "You're Always on My Mind"—about the human need for love and connection.

I am not suggesting that '90s R&B was characterized by artists upholding biblical standards of sexual ethics. Most of the songs about sex at the time were not being sung by married artists marketing their music to Christian fans. That said, many songs of that era cultivated a sense of desire and affection in the minds of listeners. Hearing young men and women talking about having a significant other on their mind and wanting to spend quality time with one another evokes a very different set of emotions than songs that are strictly about sexual conquest. A similar artistic revival is needed in television and film. *The Cosby Show*, *Family Matters*, *The Fresh Prince of Bel-Air*, *Martin*, and *Roc* are just a small sample of the television shows—in my lifetime—that demonstrated the diversity of black family life. Some depicted working-class families with fathers who were police officers and sanitation workers. Others featured mothers and fathers who worked as lawyers and doctors. All reinforced the importance of education, hard work, and a loving, stable family life.

The idea that "representation matters" plays an important role in the dissolution of the black family. The culture that surrounds us has an influence on our thoughts and actions. I find it impossible to believe that a black boy who grows up in an inner-city neighborhood enmeshed in hip-hop culture would not have his ideas about women shaped by men he has spent an entire lifetime looking up to and identifying with. Companies spend billions on advertising and recruit celebrity pitchmen because they understand the power of influence.

It is silly to believe that hip-hop artists can impact the sneakers people wear, the alcohol they drink, the clothing they buy, the jewelry they desire, and the cars they drive but *not* how they see the world.

Why would anyone expect a young black man raised by a single mother in a neighborhood where that is the norm to value marriage, especially when he has spent his entire life hearing the people he idolizes call his female counterparts "bitches" and "hoes"? Why would a young black woman value her body when the female artists she admires most brag about being sexually promiscuous and spend more time twerking than singing? Make no mistake, nonmarital birth rates were on the rise long before rap became a global phenomenon. Still, it is hard to argue that a genre that routinely describes and depicts women—particularly black women—as sexually promiscuous, disagreeable, and opportunistic has not had *any* effect on the relationship between the sexes. I don't blame music, television, and film for the breakdown of the black family, but I do believe the cultural outputs created by, directed at, and consumed by the black community have affected our ability to create and sustain a family culture built on the institution of marriage.

Conclusion

I have seen the power of positive marriage marketing up close. Lamar and Ronnie Tyler created the website Black and Married with Kids (BMWK) in 2007 to promote positive images of marriage and parenting in the black community. Their work was featured in a variety of media outlets, including *EBONY*, *Essence*, *Jet*, and *The Washington Post*. In addition to the site, the Tylers have also produced several documentaries on topics such as marriage, manhood, and wealth. As I stated before, I met my wife at a BMWK documentary screening in Washington, DC, in 2011. At the time, I was the only single man writing for the site. The Tylers attended our wedding the following year and featured it on the website.[36] They have also hosted several marriage cruises that brought couples from across the country together to help them build loving marriages and strong families. Their work is a blueprint for how technology and media can be used to reestablish a marriage and family culture in black America.

Some of the same people who would argue that hip-hop is a vehicle for setting cultural trends—both in America and across the globe—also claim that music and media have no discernible effect on the values of the people who most identify with its artists. These people are dishonest, deceived, or a combination of both. Representation cannot be critically important for some professions but completely irrelevant for others. Likewise, images of violent black men and hypersexual black women should be seen as troublesome not just when white people are the ones propagating them. In fact, I would argue that black men and women in hip-hop culture have been far more effective at promoting negative stereotypes than any Ku Klux Klan propagandist. When you know someone hates you, the natural reaction to their opinions about you is resistance. But people are far more open to receiving and accepting the values and beliefs of people with whom they identify.

For much of the twentieth century, the public image of black Americans was under constant assault from people who sought to paint the race as unintelligent, lazy, violent, and promiscuous. Even today, racist depictions of blacks from that era make people cringe. The ubiquity of these stereotypical images is why the photography of Gordon Parks, Charles "Teenie" Harris, and James Van Der Zee was so important. These men captured the everyday lives of black Americans—with their families, going to church, running businesses—in ways that displayed the *humanity* of the people in their photos, which is the very thing racial stereotypes always seek to destroy.

Black leaders in previous generations understood the power that music, film, and television have in shaping self-perception. This is why the NAACP fought *The Birth of a Nation* in the early 1900s and C. Delores Tucker criticized *Doggystyle* in the early 1990s. Unfortunately, her warnings were ignored, and over the course of the next three decades, the violence and misogyny she criticized have become essential features of hip-hop culture. Black progressive intellectuals today tend to characterize concerns about the public image of African Americans as "respectability politics." They assume that a black mother who doesn't want her teenage daughter twerking in public every time a popular song comes on is concerned about what white people might think. The black mothers I know just want to raise daughters who respect themselves and their bodies. They preach a message of self-respect, not white acceptance, because they believe respectability is a far superior cultural ideal than degeneracy.

What makes the downward spiral of hip-hop culture so disappointing is how drastically the self-destructive elements of rap depart from—and overshadow—the rich history of black American music in this country. One *City Journal* essay by Howard Husock entitled "When Black Music Was Conservative" described the messages of love, marriage, and family that permeated R&B and soul music for decades.[37] Even rappers who achieved mainstream success didn't always use their lyrics to disrespect women. LL Cool J had hit singles like "I Need Love" and "Around the Way Girl" in the "golden age" of hip-hop, typically seen as stretching from the mid-1980s to the middle of the 1990s.

The transition from music that centered on the desires of the heart to songs that are all about satisfying the flesh has had a profound effect on how black men and women relate to one another. Sowing seeds of division and disrespect will never yield a harvest of loving, intact families where men protect their wives, wives respect their husbands, and children honor their parents.

• • •

NINE

Rally Marriage
Advocates for Battle

Joy Jones is an author and artist who learned a valuable lesson about marriage while teaching elementary school students in Washington, DC. According to an opinion piece Jones wrote in *The Washington Post*, the career exploration class she taught eventually got onto the topic of family. Jones was happy when some of the boys said they looked forward to being fathers in the future. The sixth graders even said fatherhood was more important to them than money or status. She was so pleased to hear about their family aspirations that she offered to invite a few couples to talk about marriage and raising children. The boys were unenthused. One told her plainly, "We're not interested in the part about marriage. Only about how to be good fathers."[1] Another boy explained their stance with five words and jaw-dropping candor.

Marriage is for white people.[2]

Jones, a black woman, started her op-ed by noting she grew up at a time when two-parent homes were the norm in America. She said her close relationship with her own father influenced her desires for a family. In her words, "I made a conscious decision that I wanted a husband, not a live-in boyfriend and not a 'baby's daddy,' when it came my time to mate and marry."[3] And while her hope for a family had not materialized at the time of her exchange, her values remained the same.

The experience Joy Jones had that day in her classroom was not simply an interaction between a teacher and student. It was the collision of two different worlds. The backdrop was the nation's capital, colloquially known as "Chocolate City," but the sentiments expressed by these young men were not unique to the District of Columbia. Her exchange represented the black family's past meeting its present and—without intervention—its future. On one side was a woman who grew up at a time when people were *expected* to marry before having children. On the other was a boy who believed marriage was not for black people. Hers was the world of two-parent homes. His was the world of single mothers. She desired to be a wife and mother. He wanted to be a dad but not a husband.

That student would be about thirty today. He was more honest about the state of the black family in 2006 than any of the degreed social scientists and civil rights activists who claim to speak for kids like him. He clearly saw the effects of the decades-long social experiment that severed marriage from childrearing. Today in Washington, DC, 77 percent of black children are born to unmarried parents, so clearly his way of thinking spread far beyond his middle school classroom.

There was a time when every child knew the basic steps to forming a family. If they saw two of their classmates—let's call them Chris and Christina—getting along a little too well, a familiar song would break out in unison:

Chris and Christina sitting in a tree,
K-I-S-S-I-N-G.
First comes love, then comes marriage,
then comes the baby in a baby carriage!

Long before these children ever took a class in economics, they understood that marriage was the worthwhile "price" adults paid for both lifelong companionship and the privilege of raising children. Today, that script is no longer the norm. What is far more common in many neighborhoods is an arrangement where someone pays a price, but it's not the adults.

Chris and Christina staring at their screens,
T-E-X-T-I-N-G.
First comes sex, then comes baby,
then comes marriage, but that's a big maybe!

This is the reality that far too many black children are born into. Their parents have tenuous commitments to one another, which means they are deprived of the greatest privilege any child could have: to be raised in a loving home by your married biological parents. The fact that 70 percent of black children are born out of wedlock and half live with a single parent can be thought of as a widescale injustice. Children have a right to their parents, but millions of black kids are denied that right on a daily basis.

In many respects, that sixth-grade boy's declaration was a stinging rebuke of the individuals and institutions in his life that failed to model the marriage-before-carriage ideal. Parents failed to see how their relationship drama impacts their children. Policymakers failed to anticipate how their welfare policies would undermine marriage. Feminist activists failed generations of young women by selling the lie that children don't need a father in the home. Black leaders failed to address the destruction of the traditional black family. The children are the only innocent party in this entire family affair. They have no control over their circumstances of birth or the relationship dynamics of their parents. They simply want to know the answers to some basic questions, such as "Who am I?" "Where do I come from?" and "Where do I belong?"

We see the consequences of family breakdown all around us: intractable inner-city poverty, violent crime, juvenile delinquency, academic underachievement, economic despair, and a self-perpetuating cycle of babies being born to unwed parents. These are the outcomes that vex policymakers, but they don't tell the full story of how much has changed over the past sixty years. An increasing number of men, women, and children live in a world of child support orders and wage garnishment, neutral location drop-offs, splitting holidays, multiple half-siblings, vetting an ex's new boyfriend or girlfriend, and perpetual "baby mama drama." These new norms mean that many children today will have no concept of the family name, the family home, the family car, a family vacation, or even a family reunion because their definition of *family* doesn't include marriage or—far too often—fathers.

I have gone to great lengths throughout this book to place responsibility for the breakdown of the black family where it belongs, but my ultimate goal here is not to engage in a never-ending blame game. One reason is that most people don't react well to criticism. The last thing children who don't have married couples in their immediate circle need is self-absorbed adults trying to justify their behavior and defend themselves from charges of cultural neglect. No, what these—and all—children need are adults willing to do hard things on their behalf. Adults willing to put aside their pride, preferences, dreams, and desires for the sake of children. Adults willing to say, on a regular basis, "it's not about me" when asked to explain their newfound spirit of self-sacrifice.

Turning around the current state of the black family will require this individual heroism as well as a cultural revival of biblical proportions. The black leaders needed to accomplish such a tall task should think of family revival as the most important civil rights issue since the 1960s, one driven by what's best for *children* based on two indisputable truths. The first is that every child has a right to the affection, protection, and direction of the man and woman who created him or her. The second is that the ideal environment for this right to be exercised is in a loving and stable home with their married biological parents. This is *the* fight of the twenty-first century, and black family revivalists must be willing to battle anything and anyone who stands in the way. We will not rest until every child from Southeast DC to South Central LA knows one thing for certain: Marriage *is* for black people.

Why Did I Get Married?

The need for rebuilding the black family according to a biblical blueprint should not be confused with the idea that every home will look the same. Every marriage requires a man and woman in the same way every house, at a bare minimum, needs a foundation, walls, and a roof. The basic elements of the structure do not prescribe a single style, evidenced by the fact that there are ranch houses, split levels, Greek villas, gothic estates, shotgun homes, and everything in between.

Reviving the black family according to God's design doesn't negate the fact that every man and woman brings something unique to the dating market, both in terms of what they desire and what they offer to the opposite sex. There are also cultural factors that shape how black men and women in particular approach marriage and family. This includes the body types, style, and hairstyles that are considered attractive. It also includes the challenges that come from never seeing a healthy marriage up close and personal. One qualitative study of black married men found that their decision to marry was based on several factors, including the unique personal traits of their wives, their faith, timing and marital readiness, and encouragement from loved ones.[4] The same study also included barriers participants overcame before tying the knot. The participants mentioned financial stability, baggage from previous relationships, disapproval from family and friends, and the perceived loss of freedom.[5]

The reason men marry is one issue. What they look for in a wife and want in a marriage is another. Kevin Samuels, the late relationship podcaster, said most men want a woman who is "fit, feminine, friendly, cooperative and submissive."[6] One website geared to an African American audience listed the qualities men look for in a wife: honesty, sexual fulfillment, recreational companionship, physical attractiveness, domestic support, and admiration and acceptance.[7] All of these track with what I have heard from men of every background and socioeconomic status throughout my adult life. Every man knows the importance of choosing a good wife. The book of Proverbs has several verses that make it clear that a good wife is a gift from God. One verse describes an "excellent wife" as the "crown of her husband."[8] Unfortunately, the same verse says that a wife "who brings shame is like rottenness in his bones." Proverbs also paints a vivid picture of the emotional drain a nagging wife has on her home, saying that a husband would be better off living on the corner of his roof or in the desert than with a quarrelsome woman.[9]

These ancient truths still apply today. No man wants to fight the world all day on his job and then come home to a battlefield with the woman he committed to for a lifetime. This is why one of the words that comes up frequently in conversations about what men want in a relationship is "peace." That looks and sounds like an environment void of yelling, arguing, harsh tones, cursing, and physical conflict. This does not mean a couple will never disagree. It just means that differences of opinion can be expressed in a non-combative manner.

One of the issues that comes up in relationship content geared to black audiences is the notion that some black women project "masculine" energy. For some women, that term describes a harsh tone and blunt communication style. For others, being masculine is connected to being in leadership at work and being a breadwinner at home. These types of women often claim they have been forced to be masculine because of their circumstances and would turn it off for the right man.[10] Obviously, each woman is different, but conditional femininity does not sound like an appealing quality in a potential spouse. That might seem unfair, but few would argue that a man who says he mainly operates in his "feminine energy"—including how he speaks, dresses, and expresses his emotions—would be the type of guy women would find attractive.

Black women, like all women, have their own set of motivations for marriage. In times past, marriage was tied to a woman's desire for children and need for financial protection, her family and community's expectations, and larger societal norms—often influenced by religion. Those factors still exist, but the stigma of having children out of wedlock has been greatly diminished in recent decades. This does not mean black women no longer value marriage. On the contrary, one survey of single African American adults revealed that 80 percent desired to marry at some point.[11] Black respondents in other studies were more likely to say marriage is "very important" than their white counterparts.[12] Black women also desire to "marry up" by finding a spouse with more education and income.[13] The hypergamous instinct, universal across racial groups, for women to seek men who elevate their social status is one reason the topic of educated black women "dating down" and "settling" for blue-collar men or mates they outearn is so controversial. Black women also desire mates who are responsible, "spiritual," and monogamous.[14]

Despite these expressed desires, one challenge for some black women today seems to be internal tension between what they have been taught about masculinity and what they desire in a man.[15] The modern woman resists the patriarchy but bemoans the loss of chivalry and male leadership. They want men to do certain things around the home—whether cutting the grass or taking out the trash—but get uncomfortable when men look to them to fulfill certain gender-typical roles. The cruel irony of the push-pull of modernity and tradition is that most women do not desire the types of men who wear their "girl power" credentials on their sleeve. A man who looks to his lady for leadership and guidance will not be looking at her for long.

One trait that women of every background desire in a man is faithfulness. While the belief that "men are dogs" is pervasive in pop culture, surveys on marital infidelity suggest something different. The Institute for Family Studies published data from the General Social Survey that found 28 percent of black men admitted to having sex with someone other than their spouse while married.[16] That was higher than the 20 percent rate for all men.[17] The same analysis demonstrated a connection between infidelity and relationship quality. Among respondents who cheated on a spouse, 40 percent were either divorced or separated, compared with only

17 percent who were never unfaithful.[18] The connection between fidelity and longevity is good news for black women who want to find love that stands the test of time. It also benefits the children who need the love and support of both a mom and dad.

Signs a New Culture Is Taking Root

One of the most important elements of a movement to revive marriage and restore the traditional black family is the ability to measure success and celebrate progress, regardless of how incremental. The first step to doing so is understanding the appropriate time frame. A cultural shift of this magnitude will take decades, which is one reason it cannot be led by politicians who primarily think in election cycles. As things stand today, every indicator of household health suggests the black family is on life support. We have the highest nonmarital birth rates and the lowest marriage rates. Those two realities contribute to both the highest rates of abortion and single-parent homes. Getting the trendlines moving in the right direction will take time. Thankfully, rebuilding the family is not burdened with the type of ambiguity that comes along with "reimagining public safety," "smashing the patriarchy," "dismantling white supremacy," or any other progressive clarion call. Everyone knows what it means for a man to marry a woman before having children with her, and no one is confused about two people staying married for life.

Quantifying the impact of a revival movement will keep economists, sociologists, politicians, and journalists busy for years to come. For decades, social scientists have treated marriage and family structure like a means to achieving better education and economic outcomes. What they will need to do moving forward is focus on metrics that correspond with the degree to which the institution of marriage is viewed as *valuable, desirable, accessible, and indispensable* for the purpose of forming a family. Creating a culture of marriage today is largely an exercise in persuasion, conveying five messages and their underlying impact on family formation:

1. Marriage is important.

2. Getting married *before* having children is ideal.

3. You don't have to get married after you have achieved all of your life goals.

4. Marriage is meant to be a lifelong union.

5. There is nothing strange about having a large family.

That's why researchers should consider focusing on five indicators of family health that correspond to each factor: marriage rate, nonmarital birth rate, age of first marriage, divorce rate, and family size.

True revival, however, is something that must be *felt*, not just measured. The real impact of black family reconstruction will be felt in working-class neighborhoods where few children today are being raised by married parents. We will know things are starting to change for the better when the black married couples at a DC public school's family night are not just engineers and project managers but also customer service reps and bus drivers.

Another sign of family culture taking root would be an increase in couples completing premarital counseling as well as marriage enrichment activities that help strengthen their relationship. Churches overflowing with *men* leading their wives and children into the sanctuary will demonstrate that the seeds being planted in this generation are yielding fruit in the future. Success will be heard—literally—in these local assemblies as babies and toddlers fill up the pews, a reflection of couples taking the biblical mandate to be fruitful and multiply seriously despite the cultural pressure to prioritize material possessions over children. This would be a positive outcome for the black church, especially the inner-city congregations where funerals for young adults are more common than weddings.

Support for family revival does not have to be restricted exclusively to civil rights institutions. The National Basketball Players Association (NBPA) Foundation funds initiatives related to education, youth sports, and social justice. The NBPA launched a campaign called #EverydayDad back in 2015 to celebrate fatherhood.[19] There is no reason the foundation cannot revive this program and expand it to promote marriage and strong families in the cities where they play. LeBron James could be featured with his wife Savannah in the first ad along with a caption like "Every King needs a Queen. Trust me, I would know." In fact, every professional league can do something similar, especially since they can also benefit from marriage revival in this country. Intact two-parent families provide the optimal environment for passing on generational traditions, like parents taking their kids to sporting events. This is just one example of how existing relationships and assets can be leveraged to promote new messages to strengthen families.

The ultimate sign that the era of family reconstruction has been successful is when people on public transportation are as likely to assume a pregnant black woman in her mid-twenties is married as they are the pregnant Asian woman sitting beside her. This is impossible to imagine right now, but it can become the new norm once a marriage-before-carriage ethos takes root in the black community. What is seen as an exception today was the rule from the end of the Civil War through the end of the civil rights movement. This book begins with slavery's impact on the African American family because men and women today need to know that even when the flames of racism and bigotry were at their hottest, the black family was not consumed.

Conclusion

Reviving marriage and rebuilding the family may sound like abstract concepts to people who have rarely, if ever, seen a healthy, intact home up close and personal. To paraphrase a popular saying, one video shared by a couple on social media was worth a thousand words about the benefits of marriage.[20] It starts with an encouraging gospel song imploring listeners to trust God through difficult times. The rest of the post puts the song selection in proper context. The husband and wife begin dancing with their child as the video flashes back to the wife going through treatment for a serious illness, with the husband faithfully by her side. The video was a powerful reminder that there is a reason the pledge of commitment "in sickness and in health" is included in marriage vows but not child support orders or divorce decrees.

The couple serves as a testament to the biblical blueprint for marriage. Their journey shows that when a home is built on a firm foundation, it can endure the storms of life that every person—regardless of marital status—is guaranteed to encounter at some point. This does not mean all family dynamics will look the same. But my argument is that rebuilding the black family requires knowing what, on a fundamental level, has to be rebuilt, and I believe the biblical blueprint is the ideal design document. In a world where terms and definitions change every few years, it is important to ground family restoration efforts in eternal truths.

The truth is that women need husbands who faithfully love them, men need wives who respect them and bring them peace, and children need parents who understand that kids are always the collateral damage in the gender wars that break out in individual homes and across the broader culture. It will take concerted effort over multiple generations to rebuild the black family. No more can the men blame the women, the women blame the men, and both parties blame white supremacy. This abdication of responsibility must end. Both men and women have a duty to do their part in contributing to strong, stable households.

What we have today in far too many neighborhoods is the opposite: a culture of casual sex where marriage *rarely* comes before the baby carriage. All of this is why any efforts to make families stronger and more stable must begin with a biblical blueprint for the cultural practices, social norms, and policies that support marriage.

My call to action is clear: Black leaders in government, media, entertainment, education, industry, and religion must marshal their resources to provide the cultural momentum needed for a family restoration movement. The black leaders in previous generations who built institutions, empowered their communities, and fought for true freedom did not believe in waiting for anyone to save them. Neither should we. Restoring marriage to its rightful place in the home is something that must be driven by black leaders, not white liberals. This is why black elites must reprioritize how they spend their cultural, social, financial, and political capital. In short, marriage revival will require black leaders to take responsibility for the communities they come from and claim to speak for.

I openly acknowledge that this is no small task, but a revival movement would provide black elites with an opportunity to show they truly care about black lives by focusing on the relationships between the men and women who create them. To date, the Afristocracy's priorities reflect its view that the main barriers to black uplift are economic inequality and systemic racism. This is why the political priorities, academic work, editorial focus, and religious convictions of black progressives all revolve around two solutions—bigger government and better white people. That must change for black nonmarital birth rates to return to pre-1960s levels.

This will require rethinking how resources are spent. Money, time, and political power are all finite resources. So are cultural influence and righteous indignation. No person can be equally passionate about ten different issues at one time. At some point, difficult decisions about how to spend time, talent, and treasure must be made. I believe the black family would benefit from a moratorium on the types of issues that command the attention of every civil rights and racial justice organization operating today. That means no more white actors being told to take responsibility for racism, no more pastors boycotting companies for rolling back DEI programs, and no more professors demanding white people set up individual reparations accounts to atone for slavery.

Shifting the Afristocracy's current priorities to focus on strengthening the black family will not be easy. Blaming white people for everything is cathartic. The equity industrial complex is quite profitable. There is much to be gained by people pushing black oppression and victimhood. Progressive politicians run on fixing racial disparities. Local governments now have racial equity plans. Corporations pledge their fealty to social justice causes to stay in the good graces of customers and shareholders. Disparities in household wealth, K–12 education, and incarceration rates are used to justify everything from antiracist math curricula to prison abolition. That means there is a lot to lose if black elites and their white allies choose to prioritize the tangible goals of increasing marriage rates and rebuilding the family over vague plans to end racism and rid the world of all oppression. Their decisions will speak volumes about their values because only one of these options tangibly improves the lives of the people they claim to represent.

The most important part of this movement, however, is in the lives of everyday people, not the opinions of politicians and college professors. That means you—yes, *you*—can decide to do something different than you have seen in your own life. You can choose to make a marriage covenant your prerequisite for starting a family. Our culture scoffs at this idea, but no one would think of starting a business with someone without a legally binding agreement that lays out the terms of the relationship and offers protection in the event it dissolves. For the readers who are already married, the most important thing you can contribute to the revival movement is protecting your relationship and modeling the values discussed in this book. As the saying goes, "more is caught than taught," which means the example married couples provide is needed as much in our revival movement as a pro-marriage marketing campaign or political stump speech.

That doesn't mean you shouldn't promote the ideas in this book to the people in your social circles. It just means that nothing will affect more change than your lived testimony. Marriage is a life-long commitment. It gets hard at times. This is when husbands and wives also need people in their corner encouraging them to weather the storms that come their way. Likewise, married couples should be intentional about reinforcing their family values in conversations with their children. Unmarried moms and dads can also extol the benefits of marriage to their children. Doing so is neither hypocritical nor self-condemning. Some of the hardest-working students on any university campus were raised by mothers and fathers who never went to college. Parents have an innate desire to want what is best for their children, regardless of their own life decisions. No one would criticize a mom with a GED for encouraging her daughter to pursue a bachelor's degree. We should be equally supportive if the same woman says she's happy her daughter is also leaving school with an "MRS degree."

I hope this book also gives you the courage to gently ask couples who have been "playing house" for a long time the question they dread most: "So, when are you two going to get married?" This line of inquiry might lead to an awkward exchange, but cultivation requires both planting *and* pruning.

Growing a marriage culture in the black community will require difficult conversations, new political priorities, and supportive social norms.

Increasing the black marriage rate and driving down the nonmarital birth rate to pre-1960s levels will take multiple generations. Opposition will come from unexpected sources. People and institutions that profit from broken families will not be happy to see their revenue streams dry up. Politicians will lose votes. Academics and activists will see their subversive theories about gender, marriage, and the family fall out of favor. But all of these "costs" pale in comparison to what we will gain. Restoring order to the family will completely change the trajectory of black America for generations to come. Rebuilding the black family will not be easy, but creating peace in our homes today and leaving a blueprint for the children of tomorrow is certainly worth the fight.

Acknowledgments

I feel a deep sense of gratitude for the many people who contributed to this project along the way. Every question, comment, encouragement, and critique helped me ensure that my heart and mind were in the right place. If I miss anyone in the acknowledgments that follow, please charge it to my head, not my heart.

First, I want to thank my wife, Stephanie. There is no way I could have written this book without your love and support. You are the world's greatest sounding board. You helped me pair the right ideas with the right words to make sure readers hear what I mean to say. You also ensured that our home ran smoothly and our children felt loved when this project required late nights. Proverbs 18:22 says, "He who finds a wife finds a good thing and obtains favor from the Lord." I can attest to the accuracy of that statement and thank your parents, Oree and Myrtis Phillips, for raising such an exemplary daughter.

To my children—Camille, Evan, Erin, and Mason—please know that being your father is one of the greatest gifts I have ever received. You are the world's best cheerleaders, despite my flaws and imperfections. I wrote this book because I want every child to know the safety and security that comes with having a dad in the home committed to fulfilling his duties as a husband and father.

I thank my parents, Volney and Paulette Squires, for modeling love, faith, stability, and structure for me. I can write confidently about the benefits of being raised in a home with two loving parents because of a decision you made over forty years ago to commit to each other for life. For that, I am eternally grateful.

I want to thank my sister, Kaila Cage, for your constant encouragement and support. Seeing you become a wife to Gary and a mother to Caleb during my writing process made this project even more special.

I want to thank all my aunts, uncles, and cousins for showing me what family looks like. There are too many people to name individually but please know that you contributed to some of the most important moments in my life as well as some of the most important parts of this book.

One of the greatest blessings in my life is the knowledge that "family" extends beyond kin. To my brothers from three other mothers—Carlos, Davrel, and Shane—thank you for being my most trusted debate partners since childhood. I'm not afraid to stand up for what I believe because all my ideas have been put through the fire—whether in person, over the phone, or via text. Four Horsemen for life.

I thank my Grace Church of God family. Jefferson and Cynthia Bannister, you have been like second parents to me for as long as I can remember. Thank you for being a constant source of light and love. I also want to thank the families who remain part of my village to this day, including the Cummins, Springers, Herberts, and Stoutes. There are so many other people I could name who helped shape me into the man I am today. You pushed me to grow in maturity, faith, and wisdom. You know who you are, and I hope you know that I am grateful for your positive influence.

Outside of my family, no two people have done more to put me on my current path—both personal and professional—than Lamar and Ronnie Tyler. You gave me my first shot writing for public consumption. My time with Black and Married with Kids opened doors that I never anticipated. But most important, I met my wife at one of your documentary screenings back in 2011 and my life has never been the same since.

I want to thank my colleagues at the Heritage Foundation for encouraging me to write this book. To Kevin Roberts, thank you for being willing to spend precious political and social capital to save the American family. I thank Jay Richards for pushing me to be a clearer thinker, better writer, and more savvy coalition builder. Derrick Morgan and Roger Severino: thank you for your constant support and encouragement. I want to say a special thank you to Amelia, Emma, Liana, Hallie, Katherine, Vivian, and every other intern who assisted me with research.

I also want to thank Jason Whitlock for helping me become a writer worth reading. A player cannot maximize his talents without good coaching. You showed me that the same applies to writers and editors.

I am grateful for the marriage and family advocates I have had the pleasure of learning from—and working with—along the way. This is a long list, but I must say a special thank you to Katy Faust, Brad Wilcox, Bob Woodson, and Ian Rowe.

I am thankful for the pastors who have given me wise counsel and tangible examples of how God can use the church to revive the institution of marriage. Thank you to Omar Johnson, Tommy Quick, John K. Jenkins, and P. M. Smith.

I want to express my sincere gratitude to my editor, Helen Healey-Cunningham for asking whether I would consider writing a book on this topic. I also want to thank Bria Sandford and the rest of the Sentinel team for their unwavering support.

Thank you to my literary agent, Giles Anderson, for helping me crystallize the vision for this book. I must say a special thank you to Alec Torres for helping me transform my manuscript from what

would have been a good book to what I hope will be the most conse-
quential text on black family life in the twenty-first century.

Last but most important, I want to thank God, from whom all
blessings flow. I pray that the words of my mouth and the meditation
of my heart be acceptable in your sight, O Lord, my rock and my re-
deemer.

Notes

Introduction

1. "1986 Special Report: 'The Vanishing Black Family'," roundtable discussion moderated by Bill Moyers, posted March 28, 2019, by Hezakya Newz & Films, YouTube, 1:31:39, youtube.com/watch?v=_vrw416MnJ8.

2. Ibid.

3. Stephanie J. Ventura and Christine A. Bachrach, "Nonmarital Childbearing in the United States, 1940–99," *National Vital Statistics Reports* 48, no. 16 (October 18, 2000): 28, cdc.gov/nchs/data/nvsr/nvsr48/nvs48_16.pdf.

4. Ibid, 31.

5. *"Fresh Prince of Bel-Air*—Will's Father leaves," posted June 21, 2015, by Charles Bentley, YouTube, 4:41, youtube.com/watch?v=PI4M v8R0mE0.

6. Michelle J. K. Osterman et al., "Births: Final Data for 2023," *National Vital Statistics Reports*, 74, no. 1 (March 18, 2025): 28, cdc.gov/nchs/data /nvsr/nvsr74/nvsr74-1.pdf.

7. "Historical Living Arrangements of Children, Table CH-3, Living Arrangements of Black Children Under 18 Years Old: 1960 to 2023," US Census Bureau, November 2024, census.gov/data/tables/time-series /demo/families/children.html.

8. "Poverty Status of Children by Family Structure, 2021," Office of Juvenile Justice and Delinquency Program, ojjdp.ojp.gov/statistical-briefing-book /population/faqs/qa01203.

9. "Characteristics of Children's Families," National Center for Education Statistics, 2020, nces.ed.gov/programs/coe/pdf/coe_cce.pdf.

10. US Census Bureau, "Historical Marital Status Tables, Table MS-1, Marital Status of the Population 15 Years Old and Over by Sex, Race and Hispanic Origin: 1950 to Present, November 2024," census.gov/data/tables/time-series/demo/families/marital.html.

11. Melissa Kollar and Zach Scherer, "Income in the United States: 2024," *Current Population Reports*, US Census Bureau, September 2025, 3, census.gov/library/publications/2025/demo/p60-286.pdf.

12. US Census Bureau, "HINC-02. Age of Householder-Households, by Total Money Income, Type of Household, Race and Hispanic Origin of Householder. Married-Couple Families: Black Alone," last revised August 16, 2024, census.gov/data/tables/time-series/demo/income-poverty/cps-hinc/hinc-02.html.

13. US Census Bureau, "HINC-02. Age of Householder-Households, by Total Money Income, Type of Household, Race and Hispanic Origin of Householder. Female Householder, Spouse Absent: Black Alone," last revised August 16, 2024, census.gov/data/tables/time-series/demo/income-poverty/cps-hinc/hinc-02.html.

14. Nicholas Zill, "Family Still Matters for Key Indicators of Student Performance," Institute for Family Studies, April 6, 2020, ifstudies.org/blog/family-still-matters-for-key-indicators-of-student-performance.

15. Nicholas Zill and Brad Wilcox, "Strong Families, Better Student Performance: The More Things Change, the More They Remain the Same," Institute for Family Studies, August 16, 2022, ifstudies.org/blog/strong-families-better-student-performance-the-more-things-change-the-more-they-remain-the-same.

16. Brad Wilcox et al., "Less Poverty, Less Prison, More College: What Two Parents Mean for Black and White Children," Institute for Family Studies, June 17, 2021, ifstudies.org/blog/less-poverty-less-prison-more-college-what-two-parents-mean-for-black-and-white-children.

17. Binta Alleyne-Green et al., "Father Involvement, Dating Violence, and Sexual Risk Behaviors Among a National Sample of Adolescent Females," HHS Public Access, March 31, 2016, pmc.ncbi.nlm.nih.gov/articles/PMC5007216/pdf/nihms812356.pdf.

Chapter One: Slavery and the Black Family

1. U.S. Constitution article IV, section 2, clause 3, Constitution Annotated, constitution.congress.gov/browse/essay/artIV-S2-C3-1/ALDE_00013571.

2. Marian Smith Holmes, "The Great Escape from Slavery of Ellen and William Craft," *Smithsonian,* June 16, 2010, smithsonianmag.com /history/the-great-escape-from-slavery-of-ellen-and-william-craft-497960.

3. Tera W. Hunter, *Bound in Wedlock: Slave and Free Black Marriage in the Nineteenth Century* (The Belknap Press of Harvard University Press, 2017), 12.

4. Ibid.

5. Smith Holmes, "The Great Escape."

6. Ibid.

7. Ibid

8. Ibid.

9. Ibid.

10. Ibid.

11. Ibid.

12. Ibid

13. Ibid.

14. Ibid.

15. Barbara McCaskill, "William and Ellen Craft," *New Georgia Encyclopedia,* July 17, 2020, georgiaencyclopedia.org/articles/history-archaeology /william-and-ellen-craft-1824-1900-1826-1891.

16. Ibid.

17. Hunter, *Bound in Wedlock*, 67–68.

18. *Dred Scott v. Sandford*, 60 U.S. 393, 407 (1856).

19. "Missouri's Dred Scott Case, 1846–1857," Missouri State Archives, Missouri Office of the Secretary of State, accessed October 17, 2024, sos.mo.gov /archives/resources/africanamerican/scott/scott.asp.

20. *Dred Scott v. Sandford*, 60 U.S. 393, 600 (1856).

21. Hunter, *Bound in Wedlock*, 30.

22. Hunter, *Bound in Wedlock*, 26.

23. Ibid.

24. Ibid., 13.

25. Ibid., 34.

26. Ibid.

27. Ibid., 50.

28. Ibid., 51.

29. Ibid., 73.

30. *Alfred v. State*, 37 Miss. 296 (1859), courtlistener.com/opinion/8041908 /alfred-v-state.

31. Hunter, *Bound in Wedlock*, 116.

32. Hunter, *Bound in Wedlock*, 43.

33. Ibid., 52.

34. Ibid., 45.

35. Ibid., 46.

36. Ibid.

37. Ibid., 6.

38. Ibid.

39. Ibid., 45.

40. Ibid., 44–45.

41. Ibid., 45.

42. Ibid.

43. "Robert Cox Reunited with His Wife After 24 Years," *Richmond Daily Dispatch*, February 27, 1879, Last Seen: Finding Family After Slavery (website), accessed October 17, 2024, informationwanted.org/items /show/3234.

44. Ibid.

45. "Harrison Bradley and His Wife Reunite After 21 Years and Remarry," *Cincinnati Enquirer*, August 17, 1880, Last Seen: Finding Family After

Slavery (website), accessed October 17, 2024, informationwanted.org
/items/show/3238.

46. Ibid.

47. Ibid.

48. Ibid.

49. "Robert Warren and Charity Atwater Reunited and Remarried After 53
Years," *Davenport Sunday Democrat*, June 6, 1897, Last Seen: Finding Family
After Slavery (website), accessed October 17, 2024, informationwanted.org
/items/show/3244.

50. Ibid.

51. Ibid.

52. "Vina Johnson Reunited with Her Husband George Perry After 43 Years,"
The Highland Weekly News, August 14, 1873, Last Seen: Finding Family After
Slavery (website), accessed October 17, 2024, informationwanted.org
/items/show/3565.

53. Ibid.

54. Ibid

55. "Enoch Arden doctrine," Legal Information Institute, Cornell Law
School, last modified October 2022, law.cornell.edu/wex/enoch_arden
_doctrine.

56. Alfred, Lord Tennyson, "Enoch Arden," Farringford, accessed October 17,
2024, farringford.co.uk/history/tennyson/poems/enoch-arden.

57. "Unnamed Married Woman Reunited with Unnamed Former Husband,"
Alexandria Gazette, July 24, 1875, Last Seen: Finding Family After Slavery
(website), accessed October 17, 2024, informationwanted.org/items
/show/4926.

58. "Unnamed Woman Returns to Find Husband Remarried," *St. Louis Globe-
Democrat*, January 23, 1885, Last Seen: Finding Family After Slavery
(website), accessed October 23, 2024, informationwanted.org/items
/show/4945.

59. Ibid.

60. Ibid.

61. Hunter, *Bound in Wedlock*, 213.

62. Ibid., 214.

63. Ibid., 211.

64. Ibid., 224.

65. Ibid.

66. "The Freedmen's Bureau," African American Heritage, National Archives, last modified October 28, 2021, archives.gov/research/african-americans /freedmens-bureau.

67. Hunter, *Bound in Wedlock*, 233.

68. Ibid.

69. Ibid., 234.

70. Hunter, *Bound in Wedlock*, 233–234.

71. Diana B. Elliott et al., "Historical Marriage Trends from 1890–2010: A Focus on Race Differences," US Census Bureau (presentation, Population Association of America, San Francisco, May 3–5, 2012), 18–24, census.gov /content/dam/Census/library/working-papers/2012/demo/sehsd-wp2012-12 _presentation.pdf.

72. E. C. Morris, "Is the Young Negro an Improvement, Morally, on His Father?" in *Twentieth Century Negro Literature*, ed. D. W. Culp (J. L. Nichols and Co., 1902), 253.

Chapter Two: Displace Men with Welfare

1. Michael Brice-Saddler, "D.C. Sent $10,800 to Dozens of New Moms. Here's How it Changed Their Lives," *Washington Post*, February 1, 2024, washingtonpost.com/dc-md-va/2024/02/01/dc-cash-payments-mothers -pilot-program.

2. Ibid.

3. Richard Fry et al., "In a Growing Share of U.S. Marriages, Husbands and Wives Earn about the Same," Pew Research Center, April 13, 2023, pewresearch.org/social-trends/2023/04/13/in-a-growing-share-of-u-s -marriages-husbands-and-wives-earn-about-the-same.

4. Office of Policy Planning and Research, "The Negro Family: The Case for National Action," US Department of Labor, March 1965, dol.gov/general /aboutdol/history/webid-moynihan.

5. Ibid.

6. Ibid.

7. Office of Policy Planning and Research, "Chapter 2: The Negro American Family," US Department of Labor, March 1965, dol.gov/general /aboutdol/history/webid-moynihan/moynchapter2.

8. Ibid.

9. Office of Policy Planning and Research, "Chapter 3: The Roots of the Problem," US Department of Labor, March 1965, dol.gov/general /aboutdol/history/webid-moynihan/moynchapter3.

10. Ibid.

11. Ibid.

12. Ibid.

13. Ibid.

14. Ibid.

15. Office of Policy Planning and Research, "Chapter 4: The Tangle of Pathology," US Department of Labor, March 1965, dol.gov/general /aboutdol/history/webid-moynihan/moynchapter4.

16. Ibid.

17. Ibid.

18. Lyndon B. Johnson, "To Fulfill These Rights," commencement address, Howard University, June 4, 1965.

19. Ibid.

20. Ann Kallman Bixby, "Public Social Welfare Expenditures, Fiscal Years 1965–87," *Social Security Bulletin* 53, no. 2 (1990), 19, ssa.gov/policy /docs/ssb/v53n2/v53n2p10.pdf.

21. Ibid.

22. Ibid.

23. Ibid.

24. Elizabeth Lower-Basch, "Preliminary Analysis of Racial Differences in Caseload Trends and Leaver Outcomes," US Department of Health and Human Services, November 30, 2000, aspe.hhs.gov/reports/tanf-leavers -diversion-studies.

25. Ibid.

26. Michael O'Connor, "Welfare Law—Aid to Dependent Children and the Substitute Parent Regulation—The State Loses a Scapegoat, the 'Man-In-The-House," *DePaul Law Review* 18, no. 2 (1969), via.library.depaul .edu/cgi/viewcontent.cgi?article=3106&context=law-review.

27. Ibid.

28. Ibid.

29. Johnnie Tillmon, "Welfare Is a Women's Issue," *Ms. Magazine*, 1972, republished March 25, 2021, msmagazine.com/2021/03/25/welfare -is-a-womens-issue-ms-magazine-spring-1972.

30. Ibid.

31. Ibid.

32. Gene Demby, "The Mothers Who Fought to Radically Reimagine Welfare," *Code Switch*, NPR, June 9, 2019, npr.org/sections/codeswitch/2019/06 /09/730684320/the-mothers-who-fought-to-radically-reimagine-welfare.

33. "Bill Clinton Campaign Ad: A Plan to End Welfare as We Know It," *Washington Post*, August 30, 2016, washingtonpost.com/video/politics /bill-clinton-in-1992-ad-a-plan-to-end-welfare-as-we-know-it/2016/08/30 /9e6350f8-6ee0-11e6-993f-73c693a89820_video.html.

34. "Table 1-17. Number and Percent of Births to Unmarried Women, by Race: United States, 1940–98," Centers for Disease Control and Prevention, archive.cdc.gov/#/details?url=https://www.cdc.gov/nchs/data/statab /t981x17.pdf.

35. Stephanie J. Ventura and Christine A. Bachrach, "Nonmarital Childbearing in the United States, 1940–99," *National Vital Statistics Reports* 48, no. 16 (October 18, 2000): 31, cdc.gov/nchs/data/nvsr/nvsr48/nvs48_16.pdf.

36. Delano Squires, "Moving Beyond Moynihan: A New Blueprint to Revive Marriage and Rebuild the Black Family," Heritage Foundation, September 17, 2025, heritage.org/sites/default/files/2025-09/SR321_0.pdf.

37. Michelle J. K. Osterman et al., "Births: Final Data for 2023," National Vital Statistics Reports, 74, no. 1 (March 18, 2025): 28, cdc.gov/nchs/data /nvsr/nvsr74/nvsr74-1.pdf.

38. Anna Sutherland, "Marriage: A Luxury Good Accessible to All," Institute for Family Studies, October 28, 2013, ifstudies.org/blog/marriage-a -luxury-good-accessible-to-all.

39. Elizabeth Wildsmith, Jennifer Manlove, and Elizabeth Cook, "Dramatic Increase in the Proportion of Births Outside of Marriage in the United States

from 1990 to 2016," *Child Trends*, August 8, 2018, childtrends.org
/publications/dramatic-increase-in-percentage-of-births-outside-marriage
-among-whites-hispanics-and-women-with-higher-education-levels.

40. Lester Munson, "Where's Daddy? Pro Athletes Have Fathered Startling
Numbers of Out-Of-Wedlock Children," *Sports Illustrated*, May 4, 1998,
web.archive.org/web/20251021224032/https://vault.si.com/vault/1998
/05/04/paternity-ward-fathering-out-of-wedlock-kids-has-become
-commonplace-among-athletes-many-of-whom-seem-oblivious-to-the
-legal-financial-and-emotional-consequences.

41. Ibid.

42. "Table 1-17. Number and Percent of Births to Unmarried Women, by Race:
United States, 1940–93," Centers for Disease Control and Prevention, archive
.cdc.gov/www_cdc_gov/nchs/data/statab/natfinal2003.annvol1_17.pdf.

43. Munson, "Where's Daddy?"

44. Michael David Smith, "After Birth of Twins, Travis Henry Now Has 11 Kids
by 10 Women," *NBC San Diego*, March 12, 2009, nbcsandiego.com/news
/sports/fanho-after-birth-of-twins-travis-henry-now-has-11-kids-by
-10-women/1871834.

45. Jessica Finn and Darren Boyle, "'That's It. Any More Would Kill Us!'"
Overjoyed NFL Star Antonio Cromartie Welcomes His Fourteenth Child—
His Third Since Having a Vasectomy—Spread Out Across Eight Mothers,"
Daily Mail, September 8, 2017, dailymail.co.uk/news/article-4865768
/Antonio-Cromartie-welcomes-arrival-14th-child.html.

46. Elizabeth Ayoola, "Cam Newton, Father of 8, Gets Confronted for 'Selfishly'
Creating 'Broken Families,'" *Essence*, August 26, 2024, essence.com
/lifestyle/cam-newton-broken-homes.

Chapter Three: Deceive Women with Feminism

1. "theGrio with Eboni K. Williams Single Motherhood by Choice Sidebar," ,
posted July 7, 2023, by Eboni K. Williams, YouTube, 3:33, youtube.com
/watch?v=P3JtLNG8_mM.

2. Dave Quinn, "Eboni K. Williams Details Her Pregnancy Journey: Why She's
Proud to Be a 'Single Mom by Choice' (Exclusive)," *People*, June 4, 2024,
people.com/eboni-k-williams-pregnancy-journey-single-mom-by-choice
-exclusive-8658408.

3. Ibid.

4. Amber Ferguson, "America Has a Black Sperm Donor Shortage. Black
Women Are Paying the Price," *Washington Post*, October 20, 2022,
washingtonpost.com/business/2022/10/20/black-sperm-donors.

5. Ibid.

6. Ibid.

7. Ibid.

8. Kate Adach, "Making Life-Affirming Decisions: Choosing Joy, Solo Motherhood and Pound Cake," *Tapestry*, CBC Radio, January 15, 2021, cbc.ca/radio/tapestry/decisions-decisions-1.5875034/making-life -affirming-decisions-choosing-joy-solo-motherhood-pound-cake-1.5875278.

9. Lindsey Blake Churchill, "The Feminine Mystique," *Encyclopedia Britannica*, October 5, 2024, britannica.com/topic/The-Feminine-Mystique.

10. Christina Hoff Sommers, "Reconsiderations: Betty Friedan's *The Feminine Mystique*," American Enterprise Institute, September 17, 2008, aei.org /articles/reconsiderations-betty-friedans-the-feminine-mystique.

11. Gloria Steinem, "What It Would Be Like If Women Win," *Time*, August 31, 1970, time.com/archive/6814493/essay-what-it-would-be -like-if-women-win.

12. Ibid.

13. Ibid.

14. Ibid.

15. Eleanor Holmes Norton et al., *Black Women's Manifesto* (Third World Women's Alliance, 1970), 4, repository.duke.edu/dc/wlmpc /wlmms01009.

16. "Anna Julia Hayward Cooper," BC Voices, published November 29, 2021, bcvoices.org/anna-julia-haywood-cooper.

17. Anna Julia Cooper, *A Voice from the South: By a Black Woman of the South* (The Aldine Printing House, 1892), gutenberg.org/cache/epub/61741 /pg61741-images.html#Page_9.

18. Rosetta Douglass Sprague, "What Role Is the Educated Negro Woman to Play in the Uplifting of Her Race?," in *Twentieth Century Negro Literature*, ed. D. W. Culp (J. L. Nichols and Co., 1902), 162.

19. Mary Church Terrell, "What Role is the Educated Negro Woman to Play in the Uplifting of Her Race?," in *Twentieth Century Negro Literature*, 166.

20. Dorothy Height quoted in "Report on Four Consultations," President's Commission on the Status of Women, October 1963, 35, files.eric.ed .gov/fulltext/ED020357.pdf.

21. The Nannie Helen Burroughs Project: Rebuilding a Culture of Character (website), nburroughsinfo.org.

22. Eleanor Holmes Norton et al., *Black Women's Manifesto*, 23.

23. Ibid.

24. Ibid.

25. Combahee River Collective, *The Combahee River Collective Statement* (Combahee River Collective, 1977), blackpast.org/african-american -history/combahee-river-collective-statement-1977.

26. Patricia Hill Collins, *Black Feminist Thought*, second edition (New York and London: Routledge, 2000), 157, negrasoulblog.wordpress.com/wp-content /uploads/2016/04/patricia-hill-collins-black-feminist-thought.pdf.

27. Ibid.

28. Norton et al., *Black Women's Manifesto*, 20.

29. Brittney Cooper, "The Big Father Figure Lie: Race, the Kardashians and the Latest War on Black Moms," *Salon*, October 7, 2015, salon.com/2015 /10/07/a_tale_of_two_magazine_covers_the_kardashians_the_lowes _americas_racist_double_standards.

30. Isheka N. Harrison, "Radical Feminist Rutgers Professor Brittany Cooper Claims We Don't Need Black Nuclear Family to Thrive, Black America Responds," *Moguldom Nation*, December 6, 2021, moguldom.com /384366/radical-feminist-rutgers-professor-brittany-cooper-claims-we-dont -need-black-nuclear-family-to-thrive-black-america-responds.

31. Gene Demby, "The Mothers Who Fought to Radically Reimagine Welfare," *Code Switch*, NPR, June 9, 2019, npr.org/sections/codeswitch/2019/06 /09/730684320/the-mothers-who-fought-to-radically-reimagine-welfare.

32. "Black-American Members by Congress," United States House of Representatives, history.house.gov/Exhibitions-and-Publications /BAIC/Historical-Data/Black-American-Representatives-and-Senators-by -Congress/.

33. "Membership of the 118th Congress: A Profile," Congressional Research Service, Updated September 12, 2024, crsreports.congress.gov/product /pdf/R/R47470.

34. "Here's How the Number of Black Americans in Congress Has Tripled Over 30 Years," USAFacts, March 22, 2023, usafacts.org/articles/heres-how -the-number-of-black-americans-in-congress-has-tripled-over-30-years.

35. es3ados (@esiiiados), "@TheView 'Ridiculous, crazy, Black men,'" X, October 13, 2024, x.com/esiiiados/status/1845645764237644252.

36. "Are Black Men the Key to Stacey Abrams Becoming Georgia's Next Governor?," roundtable discussion moderated by Tiffany Cross, September 17, 2022, posted by MSNBC, YouTube, 10:00, youtube.com/watch?v=arxouyu GdRw.

37. Roland Martin (@rolandsmartin), "Y'all know I've got LOTS to say about that BS event Donald Trump had at a Black church in Detroit.," Instagram, June 17, 2024, instagram.com/p/C8VT9a2vyTQ.

38. "History of Planned Parenthood," Planned Parenthood, accessed October 22, 2024, plannedparenthood.org/about-us/who-we-are/our-history.

39. "A Timeline of Contraception," *American Experience*, accessed October 22, 2024, pbs.org/wgbh/americanexperience/features/pill-timeline.

40. bell hooks, *Feminism Is for Everybody* (South End Press, 2000), 26.

41. Fabiola Cineas, "Black Women Will Suffer the Most Without *Roe*," *Vox*, June 29, 2022, vox.com/2022/6/29/23187002/black-women-abortion -access-roe.

42. Erin Aubry Kaplan, "I'm Black. I Thought White Feminism Would Keep Abortion Safe," *Politico*, May 27, 2022, politico.com/news /magazine/2022/05/27/abortion-feminism-essay-white-black -00032987.

43. "Table 9: Live Births by Race/Ethnicity and Resident County New York State 2016," Department of Health, last updated May 2018, www.health .ny.gov/statistics/vital_statistics/2016/table09.htm; "Table 23: Induced Abortion and Abortion Ratios by Race/Ethnicity and Resident County New York State—2016," Department of Health, last updated May 2018, health.ny.gov/statistics/vital_statistics/2016/table23.htm.

44. Tessa Cox, "Abortion Reporting: New York City (2019)," Charlotte Lozier Institute, June 7, 2022, lozierinstitute.org/abortion-reporting-new-york -city-2019.

45. Katherine Kortsmit et al., "Abortion Surveillance—United States, 2021," *Morbidity and Mortality Weekly Report* 72, no. 9 (Centers for Disease Control and Prevention, November 2023), 19, cdc.gov/mmwr/volumes/72/ss /pdfs/ss7209a1-H.pdf.

46. Ibid., 20.

47. Rachel MacNair, "'Is It Too Late?' 1971 Speech of Fannie Lou Hamer," *Consistent Life Blog*, February 6, 2018, consistent-life.org/blog/index .php/2018/02/06/fannie-lou-hamer.

48. "Mildred Jefferson Addresses the National Right to Life Conference," Harvard Radcliffe Institute, October 21, 2020, radcliffe.harvard.edu /news-and-ideas/mildred-jefferson-addresses-the-national-right-to-life -conference.

49. Robert E. Johnson, "Legal Abortion: Is It Genocide or Blessing in Disguise?," *Jet*, March 22, 1973, 15, books.google.com/books?id=5bEDAAAAMBAJ &lpg=PA1&pg=PA15#v=onepage&q&f=false.

50. Ibid., 16.

51. Elaine Brown, *A Taste of Power: A Black Woman's Story* (Anchor Books, 1993), 368; "Brief History of Black Americans Fighting for Reproductive Rights and Justice," Planned Parenthood of Delaware, February 19, 2019, plannedparenthood.org/planned-parenthood-delaware/blog /brief-history-of-black-americans-fighting-for-reproductive-rights-and -justice.

52. Rebecca Walker, "How My Mother's Fanatical Views Tore Us Apart," *Daily Mail*, May 23, 2008, dailymail.co.uk/femail/article-1021293/How -mothers-fanatical-feminist-views-tore-apart-daughter-The-Color-Purple -author.html.

53. Ibid.

54. Ibid.

55. Ibid.

56. "Degrees Conferred by Race/Ethnicity and Sex," National Center for Education Statistics, April 4, 2024, nces.ed.gov/fastfacts/display.asp ?id=72.

57. "Usual Weekly Earnings of Wage and Salary Workers First Quarter 2025," Bureau of Labor Statistics, US Department of Labor, April 16, 2025, bls.gov/news.release/pdf/wkyeng.pdf.

58. Lawrence Yun et al., "2023 Snapshot of Race and Home Buying in America," National Association of REALTORS Research Group, 28, nar.realtor /sites/default/files/documents/2023-snapshot-of-race-and-home-buying-in -the-us-03-02-2023.pdf.

59. Kendall Tietz, "Marriage Promotes 'White Supremacy,' According to White University Professor," Fox News, March 15, 2024, foxnews.com/media/marriage-promotes-white-supremacy-university-professor.

60. Yeris Mayol-Garcis et al., "Historical Marital Status Tables,", *Current Population Reports* (April 2021), 7, Table MS-1: Number, Timing, and Duration of Marriages and Divorces: 2016, census.gov/content/dam/Census/library/publications/2021/demo/p70-167.pdf.

61. Horowitz et al., "The Landscape of Marriage and Cohabitation in the U.S.,"; "Percent of Households by Race and Hispanic Origin of the Householder, 2023," US Census Bureau, 2023, Figure HH-7a, census.gov/content/dam/Census/library/visualizations/time-series/demo/families-and-households/hh-7a.pdf.

62. Elizabeth Ayoola, "Stop Criticizing Tia Mowry and Women Like Her for Leaving 'Good' Men," *Essence*, May 17, 2024, essence.com/lifestyle/tia-mowry-boyfriend-2024.

Chapter Four: Deny There's a Problem

1. "The Untreated Syphilis Study at Tuskegee Timeline," Centers for Disease Control and Prevention, September 4, 2024, cdc.gov/tuskegee/about/timeline.html

2. Neelam Bohra and Christina Zdanowicz, "A Black Man Feared the Vaccine Because of the Tuskegee Experiment. After Covid-19 Devastated His Family, He Changed His Mind," CNN, August 2, 2021, cnn.com/2021/08/02/us/tuskegee-experiment-covid-vaccine-hesitancy-trnd/index.html.

3. Mythinformed, (@Mythinformed MKE), "'It's my job to diagnose racism. It's my job to provide treatments.' Ibram X Kendi equates his job as a Woke 'anti-racist' author to an actual medical doctor for an auditorium full of middle school students," X, March 14, 2024, x.com/MythinformedMKE/status/1768274672406171941.

4. W. E. B. DuBois, "The Talented Tenth," in *The Negro Problem*, ed. Booker T. Washington (1903), gutenberg.org/cache/epub/15041/pg15041-images.html#The_Talented_Tenth.

5. Ibid.

6. Ibid.

7. C. H. Turner, "Will the Education of the Negro Solve the Race Problem?," in *Twentieth Century Negro Literature*, ed. D. W. Culp (J. L. Nichols and Co., 1902), 157.

8. Michael Eric Dyson, *Is Bill Cosby Right? Or Has the Black Middle Class Lost Its Mind?* (Basic Civitas Books, 2005), xi–xii.

9. Ibid.

10. Ibid., xiii.

11. Ibid., xiv.

12. Chris Gardner, "NAACP, Hollywood Stars Partner for 'I Take Responsibility' PSA Addressing Unchecked Racism," *Hollywood Reporter*, June 11, 2020, hollywoodreporter.com/news/general-news/naacp -hollywood-stars-partner-i-take-responsibility-psa-1297927.

13. "Dyson: Whites Should Open Individual Reparations Accounts," posted October 23, 2024, by Fox News, YouTube, 5:53, youtu.be /95tC328G51Q.

14. Michael Harriot, "Why We Never Talk about Black-on-Black Crime: An Answer to White America's Most Pressing Question," *The Root*, October 3, 2017, theroot.com/why-we-never-talk-about-black-on-black-crime-an -answer-to-white-americas-most-pressing-question.

15. Delano Squires, "Moving Beyond Moynihan: A New Blueprint to Revive Marriage and Rebuild the Black Family," Heritage Foundation, September 17, 2025, heritage.org/sites/default/files/2025-09/SR321_0.pdf.

16. "Michael Eric Dyson Attacks Don Lemon, O'Reilly: What About 'Pathology at Heart of the White Family?'," posted July 30, 2013, by Martysoffice, YouTube, 4:34, youtu.be/M_Ox86iCfVw.

17. Ivory A. Toldson, "Single Parents Aren't the Problem," *Root*, July 3, 2013, theroot.com/single-parents-arent-the-problem-1790897125.

18. Melissa Harris-Perry, "*The Melissa Harris-Perry Show* for Sunday, July 27th, 2014," NBC News, February 2, 2017, nbcnews.com/id/wbna55740123.

19. Mary Parke, "Are Married Parents Really Better for Children?," *Couples and Marriage Research and Policy Brief*, (Center for Law and Social Policy, 2023), 2, clasp.org/sites/default/files/public/resources-and-publications/states /0086.pdf.

20. Christina J. Cross, *Inherited Inequality: Why Opportunity Gaps Persist Between Black and White Youth Raised in Two-Parent Families* (Harvard University Press, 2025), 21.

21. "TX Abortion Law 'Creates Vigilante System': SCOTUS Refuses to Block New Controversial Abortion Law," posted September 5, 2021, by Roland S. Martin, YouTube, 22:51, youtube.com/watch?v=dtdBC6LM5xc.

22. Charles M. Blow, "Black Dads Are Doing Best of All," *New York Times*, June 8, 2015, nytimes.com/2015/06/08/opinion/charles-blow-black-dads -are-doing-the-best-of-all.html.

23. Jo Jones and William D. Mosher, "Fathers' Involvement with Their Children: United States, 2006–2010," *National Health Statistics Reports* 71, National Center for Health Statistics, December 20, 2013, cdc.gov/nchs/data/nhsr /nhsr071.pdf.

24. Ibid.

25. Ibid.

26. Ibid.

27. Delano Squires, "Moving Beyond Moynihan."

28. Paul Hemez and Chanell Washington, "Percentage and Number of Children Living with Two Parents Has Dropped Since 1968," United States Census Bureau, April 12, 2021, census.gov/library/stories/2021/04/number-of -children-living-only-with-their-mothers-has-doubled-in-past-50-years.html.

29. Barack Obama, "Remarks by the President On Strengthening the Economy for the Middle Class," White House, February 15, 2013, obamawhitehouse .archives.gov/the-press-office/2013/02/15/remarks-president-strengthening -economy-middle-class.

30. Brittney C. Cooper, "Mr. President, Stop Throwing Black People Under the Bus," *Ebony*, February 18, 2013, ebony.com/mr-president-stop-throwing -black-people-under-the-bus-305.

Chapter Five: Distort the Bible for Political Power

1. "Barack Obama on Gay Marriage," posted October 28, 2008, Glassboothdotorg, youtube.com/watch?v=N6K9dS9wl7U.

2. Barack Obama, interview by Rick Warren, August 16, 2008, Saddleback Presidential Candidates Forum, CNN Transcripts, transcripts.cnn .com/show/se/date/2008-08-16/segment/02.

3. Phil Gast, "Obama Announces he Supports Same-Sex Marriage," CNN Politics, May 9, 2012, cnn.com/2012/05/09/politics/obama-same-sex -marriage/index.html.

4. Ibid.

5. Rev. Al Sharpton et al., "Open Letter Embracing President Obama's Position on Equality for Gay & Lesbian Individuals," National Action Network, May 11,

2012, nationalactionnetwork.net/press/open-letter-embracing
-president-obamas-position-on-equality-for-gay-lesbian-individuals.

6. Ibid.

7. Otis Moss, "Otis Moss, III Challenges Fellow Black Clergy on Marriage
Equality for Gays and Lesbians," *HuffPost*, May 28, 2012, huffpost.com
/entry/otis-moss-iii-challenges-on-marriage-equality_n_1550449.

8. Ibid.

9. Raphael Warnock, "Senator Reverend Warnock Statement on the Senate
Passage of the Bipartisan Respect for Marriage Act," Reverend Raphael
Warnock US Senator for Georgia, November 29, 2022, warnock.senate.gov
/newsroom/press-releases/senator-reverend-warnock-statement-on-the-senate
-passage-of-the-bipartisan-respect-for-marriage-act.

10. Besheer Mohamed et al., "Faith Among Black Americans," Pew Research
Center, February 16, 2021, 152, pewresearch.org/wp-content/uploads
/sites/20/2021/02/PF_02.16.21_Black.religion.report.pdf.

11. Ibid., 153.

12. Ibid.

13. Albert J. Raboteau, *Slave Religion: The "Invisible Institution" in the
Antebellum South*, first ed. (Oxford University Press, 2004), 212,
southinblackandwhite.wordpress.com/wp-content/uploads/2011/01
/raboteau_slave-religion.pdf.

14. Ibid., 213–214.

15. Ibid., 214.

16. Ibid.

17. Besheer Mohamed et al., "Faith Among Black Americans," 153.

18. Ibid.

19. Ibid.

20. J. B. L. Williams, "To What Extent Is the Negro Pulpit Uplifting the Race?,"
in *Twentieth Century Negro Literature*, ed. D. W. Culp (J. L. Nichols and Co.,
1902), 114–115.

21. "Bishop B.W. Arnett," *African American Perspectives: Materials Selected from
the Rare Book Collection*, Library of Congress, accessed October 23, 2024,
loc.gov/collections/african-american-perspectives-rare-books/articles
-and-essays/daniel-murray-a-collectors-legacy/bishop-b-w-arnett.

22. J. B. L. Williams, "To What Extent Is the Negro Pulpit Uplifting the Race?"

23. Martin Luther King Jr., "The Crisis in the Modern Family," sermon, Dexter Avenue Baptist Church, May 8, 1955, Martin Luther King, Jr. Research and Education Institute, kinginstitute.stanford.edu/king-papers/documents/crisis -modern-family-sermon-dexter-avenue-baptist-church.

24. James H. Cone, *A Black Theology of Liberation* (Lippincott, 1970), 25.

25. Ibid.

26. James H. Cone, *For My People: Black Theology and the Black Church* (Maryknoll, 1984), 92–93.

27. Woke Preacher Clips (@WokePreacherTV), "James Cone: If You Exclude 'Queer People' From Church, 'You Are Just As Guilty' As People Who Lynched Black Men," X, June 20, 2025, x.com/WokePreacherTV /status/1936055973556228370.

28. Clyde McGrady and Lateshia Beachum, "Why Some Black Churches Aren't Elated About the Possible End of *Roe*," *Washington Post*, May 13, 2022, washingtonpost.com/lifestyle/2022/05/13/roe-abortion-black -church.

29. Ibid.

30. Ibid.

31. Ibid.

32. Pastorhjw (@pastorhjw), "In honor of Flashback Friday," Instagram, July 15, 2022, instagram.com/p/CgDUlS9Olhv.

33. Kevin Freking, "President Obama and Family Attend Easter Service at Historic Alfred Street Baptist Church," ABC7 News, March 27, 2016, wjla.com/news/local/president-obama-and-family-attend-easter -service-at-historic-alfred-street-baptist-church; Fleur Paysour, "Alfred Street Baptist Church Donates $1 Million to National Museum of African American History and Culture," Smithsonian National Museum of African American History and Culture, November 9, 2015, si.edu/newsdesk /releases/alfred-street-baptist-church-donates-1-million-national-museum -african-american-history-and.

34. Woke Preacher Clips (@WokePreacherTV), "Jamal H. Bryant, pastor of an Atlanta-area church named 'New Birth,' delivers a pro-choice stump speech," X, July 1, 2022, x.com/wokepreachertv/status/15428825585931 87840.

Interlude: A New Era

1. Crystal Ponti, "America's History of Slavery Began Long Before Jamestown," *History*, August 14, 2019, history.com/articles/american-slavery-before-jamestown-1619.

2. Diana B. Elliott et al., "Historical Marriage Trends from 1890–2010: A Focus on Race Differences," US Census Bureau (presentation, Population Association of America, San Francisco, May 3–5, 2012), 18–24, census.gov/content/dam/Census/library/working-papers/2012/demo/SEHSD-WP2012-12.pdf.

3. Stephanie J. Ventura and Christine A. Bachrach, "Nonmarital Childbearing in the United States, 1940–99," *National Vital Statistics Reports* 48, no. 16 (October 18, 2000): 31, cdc.gov/nchs/data/nvsr/nvsr48/nvs48_16.pdf.

4. "Perinatal Health and Infant Mortality Report," Center for Policy Planning and Evaluation Community Health Administration, District of Columbia Department of Health, 2022, dchealth.dc.gov/sites/default/files/dc/sites/doh/publication/attachments/2022-07-CPPE-PHIMreport-9-web.pdf.

Chapter Six: Reframe the Issue for Key Institutions

1. Juliana Menasce Horowitz et al., "2. Public Views of Marriage and Cohabitation," Pew Research Center, November 6, 2019, pewresearch.org/social-trends/2019/11/06/public-views-of-marriage-and-cohabitation.

2. Gen 2:15 (ESV).

3. 1 Tm 5:8 (ESV).

4. Adam Pearce and Dorothy Gambrell, "This Chart Shows Who Marries CEOs, Doctors, Chefs, and Janitors," *Bloomberg*, February 11, 2016, bloomberg.com/graphics/2016-who-marries-whom.

5. Richard Fry et al., "In a Growing Share of U.S. Marriages, Husbands and Wives Earn About the Same," Pew Research Center, April 13, 2023, pewresearch.org/social-trends/2023/04/13/in-a-growing-share-of-u-s-marriages-husbands-and-wives-earn-about-the-same.

6. Ibid.

7. Ti. 2:4–5 (ESV).

8. Honor Jones, "How I Demolished My Life," *Atlantic*, December 28, 2021, theatlantic.com/family/archive/2021/12/divorce-parenting/621054.

9. Eph 5:22–24 (ESV).

10. Eph 5:25–29 (ESV).

11. Wendy Wang and Brad Wilcox, "The Power of the Success Sequence for Disadvantaged Young Adults," Institute for Family Studies, May 2022, 2, ifstudies.org/ifs-admin/resources/reports /successsequencedisadvantagedya-final.pdf.

12. Nat Malkus, "Uncommonly Popular: Public Support for Teaching the Success Sequence in School," AEI, December 2021, aei.org/wp -content/uploads/2021/12/Uncommonly-Popular.pdf?x85095.

13. "Mayor Adams Statement on Drag Storytelling," June 16, 2022, nyc.gov /office-of-the-mayor/news/408-22/mayor-adams-on-drag-storytelling.

14. Ian M. Giatti, "Most Parents Say 'Drag Queen Story Hour' Events are Inappropriate for Children: Poll," *Christian Post*, November 23, 2022, christianpost.com/news/most-parents-say-drag-queen-events-are -inappropriate-for-kids.html.

15. Paul Hemez and Chanell Washington, "Percentage and Number of Children Living With Two Parents Has Dropped Since 1968," United States Census Bureau, April 12, 2021, census.gov/library/stories/2021/04/number-of -children-living-only-with-their-mothers-has-doubled-in-past-50 -years.html.

16. Michelle Castillo, "New York's Teen Pregnancy PSAs," CBS News, March 4, 2013, cbsnews.com/pictures/new-yorks-teen-pregnancy-psas/3.

17. Michelle Singletary, "Being a Teen Parent Will Cost You," *Washington Post*, March 14, 2013, washingtonpost.com/business/economy/being-a-teen -parent-will-cost-you/2013/03/14/434b51c8-8cb4-11e2-b63f-f53fb9f2fcb4 _story.html.

18. "Helping Every Area of Relationships Thrive—Adults (HEART)," Department of Health and Human Services Administration for Children and Families, grants.gov/search-results-detail/355694.

Chapter Seven: Remove Political Obstacles

1. "What We Believe," Black Lives Matter, web.archive.org/web /20190930154938/https://blacklivesmatter.com/what-we-believe.

2. "Black Lives Matter Foundation Statement on Supreme Court Ruling Overturning Roe," Black Lives Matter, June 24, 2022, blacklivesmatter.com /black-lives-matter-global-network-foundation-statement-on-supreme -court-ruling-overturning-roe.

3. Sony Salzman, "From the Start, Black Lives Matter Has Been About LGBTQ Lives," ABC News, June 21, 2020, abcnews.go.com/US /start-black-lives-matter-lgbtq-lives/story?id=71320450; "What We Believe," Black Lives Matter.

4. Jacob Channel, "Homeownership Gender Gap: Single Women Own More Homes Than Single Men," Lending Tree, January 27, 2025, lendingtree.com /home/mortgage/single-women-own-more-homes-than-single -men-do.

5. "Degrees Conferred by Postsecondary Institutions, by Level of Degree and Sex of Student: Selected Years, 1869–70 Through 2029–30," National Center for Education Statistics, nces.ed.gov/programs/digest/d20/tables /dt20_318.10.asp?current=yes.

6. "Degrees Conferred by Race/Ethnicity and Sex," National Center for Education Statistics, April 4, 2024, nces.ed.gov/fastfacts/display.asp ?id=72.

7. USA TODAY (@USATODAY), "After George Floyd's death, corporate America pledged to improve diversity in hiring . . . ," X, May 25, 2022, x.com/usatoday/status/1529590885922402304.

8. Diana B. Elliott et al., "Historical Marriage Trends from 1890–2010: A Focus on Race Differences," US Census Bureau (presentation, Population Association of America, San Francisco, May 3–5, 2012), 24, census.gov /content/dam/Census/library/working-papers/2012/demo/SEHSD -WP2012-12.pdf.

9. Yeris Mayol-Garcis et al., "Number, Timing, and Duration of Marriages and Divorces: 2016," April 2021, 7, census.gov/content/dam/Census/library /publications/2021/demo/p70-167.pdf.

10. Scott Roberts, "The Biblical Order of the Family, and Dispelling Misconceptions About It," Scott Roberts, February 12, 2019, accessed November 8, 2024, scottroberts.org/the-biblical-order-of-the-family -and-dispelling-misconceptions-about-it.

11. Rebecca Traister, "The Return of the Marriage Plot," *The Cut*, September 22, 2023, thecut.com/article/why-is-everyone-so-eager-for-men-and -women-to-get-married.html.

12. Katherine Kortsmit et al., "Abortion Surveillance—United States, 2021," Centers for Disease Control and Prevention, November 24, 2023, 20, cdc.gov /mmwr/volumes/72/ss/pdfs/ss7209a1-H.pdf.

13. Emily Wagster Pettis and Leah Willingham, "Black and Hispanic People Have the Most to Lose if *Roe* is Overturned," *PBS NewsHour*, May 4, 2022, pbs.org/newshour/nation/black-and-hispanic-people-have-the-most-to-lose-if-roe-is-overturned.

14. Sandhya Dirks, "Abortion is Also About Racial Justice, Experts and Advocates Say," NPR, June 27, 2022, npr.org/2022/05/14/1098306203/abortion-is-also-about-racial-justice-experts-and-advocates-say.

15. Katherine Kortsmit et al, "Abortion Surveillance—United States, 2021," 6.

16. Ibid., 19.

17. "About Us," NBJC, nbjc.org/nbjcabout-us.

18. "The Breakfast Club Address Trans Issues With Malik Yoba, Carmen Carrera, David Johns + Nala Simone," posted September 11, 2019, by The Breakfast Club Power 105.1 FM, YouTube, 1:12:11, youtube.com/watch?v=pBAFhcDQmnA&t=3960s.

19. Dave Zirin, "Tony Dungy Is a Right-Wing Zealot and the NFL and NBC Don't Care," *Nation*, January 19, 2023, thenation.com/article/society/tony-dungy-march-life.

20. Nancy Armour, "Tony Dungy Shows His True Values with Hateful Tweet That Puts Transgender Kids at Risk," *USA Today*, January 19, 2023, usatoday.com/story/sports/columnist/nancy-armour/2023/01/19/tony-dungy-bigotry-vulnerable-transgender-kids-risk/11085306002.

21. Soon Kyu Choi et al., "Black LGBT Adults in the U.S.: LGBT Well-Being at the Intersection of Race," Williams Institute, UCLA School of Law, January 2021, williamsinstitute.law.ucla.edu/publications/black-lgbt-adults-in-the-us.

22. Paul F. Hemez et al., "America's Families and Living Arrangements: 2022," *Current Population Reports*, US Census Bureau, May 2024, 10, census.gov/library/publications/2024/demo/p20-587.pdf.

23. "Racial and Ethnic Composition," Pew Research Center, pewresearch.org/religious-landscape-study/database/racial-and-ethnic-composition.

24. Gregory A. Smith et al., "Religious 'Nones' in America: Who They Are and What They Believe," Pew Research Center, January 24, 2024, 87, pewresearch.org/wp-content/uploads/sites/20/2024/01/PR_2024.01.24_religious-nones_REPORT.pdf.

25. Besheer Mohamed et al., "Faith Among Black Americans," 88.

26. Kiley Hurst, "Rising Share of Americans See Women Raising Children on Their Own, Cohabitation as Bad for Society," Pew Research Center, March 11, 2022, pewresearch.org/short-reads/2022/03/11/rising-share-of -americans-see-women-raising-children-on-their-own-cohabitation-as-bad -for-society.

27. Paul Hemez and Chanell Washington, "Percentage and Number of Children Living with Two Parents Has Dropped since 1968," United States Census Bureau, April 12, 2021, census.gov/library/stories/2021/04/number-of -children-living-only-with-their-mothers-has-doubled-in-past-50-years.html.

28. Juliana Horowitz et al., "Marriage and Cohabitation in the U.S.," Pew Research Center, November 6, 2019: 18, 22, pewresearch.org/wp -content/uploads/sites/20/2019/11/PSDT_11.06.19_marriage_cohabitation _FULL.final_.pdf.

29. Stephanie Saul, "An Ambitious Antiracism Center Scales Back Amid Allegations of Poor Management," *New York Times*, September 23, 2023, nytimes.com/2023/09/23/us/ibram-x-kendi-antiracism-boston -university.html.

30. Barbara VanDenburgh, "Anti-Racist Book Dethrones *Hunger Games* Prequel on Best-seller List amid Mass Protests," *USA Today*, June 10, 2020, usatoday.com/story/entertainment/books/2020/06/10/anti-racist-books -dominate-best-seller-list-white-fragility-how-to-be-an-antiracist-ta-nehisi -coates/5331188002.

31. "Districtwide Racial Equity Action Plan," Mayor's Office of Racial Equity, District of Columbia Government, 2024, 34, ore.dc.gov/sites/default /files/dc/sites/ore/page_content/attachments/ORE-REAP-2024-a.pdf.

32. Jessica Chasmar, "Ben Crump Panned for Praising the Removal of 'Master Bedroom' from Minnesota Real Estate Listings," Fox News, August 10, 2021, foxnews.com/politics/ben-crump-panned-removal-master -bedroom-minnesota-real-estate.

33. John Kass, "What was Marx's Position on High-End Real Estate? Ask BLM's Patrisse Khan-Cullors," *Chicago Tribune*, April 15, 2021, chicagotribune.com/2021/04/15/column-what-was-marxs-position-on -high-end-real-estate-ask-blms-patrisse-khan-cullors.

Chapter Eight: Reject Destructive Media

1. National Rainbow Coalition, "Violence Against Women," C-SPAN, January 6, 1994, 23:35–35:15, c-span.org/program/public-affairs-event/violence-against -women/42399.

2. Ibid.

3. Ibid.

4. Ibid.

5. Ibid.

6. Chuck Philips, "Anti-Rap Crusader Under Fire," *Los Angeles Times*, March 20, 1996, latimes.com/local/la-fi-tupacdelores20march2096 -story.html.

7. Ibid.

8. "Rap Game (Solo Mix)," track 12 on Eminem, *Don't Call Me Marshall*, Interscope Records, 2003.

9. National Rainbow Coalition, "Violence Against Women."

10. Lindsey E. Mccormack, "Professor Shaped Eight Years Of 'Cosby'," *Harvard Crimson*, May 24, 2022, thecrimson.com/article/2002/5/24/professor -shaped-eight-years-of-cosby.

11. Ibid.

12. "D.W. Griffith's *The Birth of a Nation*," PBS, pbs.org/wgbh/cultureshock /flashpoints/theater/birthofanation.html.

13. Wormser, Richard, "D.W. Griffith's *The Birth of a Nation* (1915)," Thirteen, thirteen.org/wnet/jimcrow/stories_events_birth.html.

14. *The Realization of a Negro's Ambition*, film poster, 1915, National Humanities Center, nationalhumanitiescenter.org/pds/maai2/forward/text5 /ambition.pdf.

15. "*The Realization of a Negro's Ambition*," IMDB, accessed December 18, 2025, imdb.com/title/tt0007251.

16. "Oscar Micheaux," Kennedy Center, accessed December 18, 2025, kennedy-center.org/education/resources-for-educators/classroom-resources /media-and-interactives/artists/micheaux-oscar.

17. "Spike Lee on *Birth of a Nation*'s Horrific Social Effects, Jordan Peele, More" interview with Jaleesa Lashay, posted August 3, 2018, by BlackTree TV, YouTube, 3:54, youtube.com/watch?v=LAIL8ZbTJVI.

18. Stephanie Victoria (@CrownVictoria22), "This is your friendly reminder that Uncle Snoop . . . ," X, March 4, 2020, x.com/CrownVictoria22/status /1235252677564682247.

19. David L. Hudson Jr. "Luke Records v. Navarro (11th Cir.) (1992)," Free Speech Center at Middle Tennessee State University, last updated July 2, 2024, firstamendment.mtsu.edu/article/luke-records-v-navarro-11th-cir.

20. "Billboard Hot 100 Week of March 20, 1993," *Billboard*, billboard.com/charts/hot-100/1993-03-20.

21. "People Everyday (LP Version)," by Todd Thomas and Sylvester Stewart, produced by Speech, Chrysalis Records, 1992.

22. "Billboard Hot 100 Week of October 10, 1992," *Billboard*, billboard.com/charts/hot-100/1992-10-10.

23. Sytonia Reid, "Revisiting C. Delores Tucker's War on Rap: Too Much Smoke, Not Enough Flowers," Sytonia Reid (blog), September 17, 2023, medium.com/@sytonia.reid11/revisiting-c-delores-tuckers-war-on-rap-too-much-smoke-not-enough-flowers-9f2ab175e0d1.

24. "U.N.I.T.Y.," by Dana Owens and Kier Gist, performed by Queen Latifah, produced by KayGee, Motown Records, released as a single on November 9, 1993.

25. Robby Starbuck (@robbystarbuck), "Exhibit A proving my point that WAP by Cardi B is degrading trash poisoning the minds of our youth," X, August 11, 2020, x.com/robbystarbuck/status/1293036419972292608.

26. Rap Alert (@rapalert6), "Sexyy Red performs 'Pound Town' live for UPROXX," X, June 16, 2023, x.com/rapalert6/status/1669901016907542532.

27. #boycottsororitysisters, X, January 2015, x.com/hashtag/boycottsororitysisters.

28. "Joe Scarborough, Mika Brzezinski, Roland Martin Talk VH1's Ratchet New Reality Show Sorority Sisters," posted December 19, 2014, by Roland S. Martin, YouTube, youtube.com/watch?v=6lVl8lQ3NmM.

29. "K Michelle Speaks Out On VH1's *Sorority Sisters*," interview with KiKi Brown, posted December 16, 2014, by RadioOne Baltimore, YouTube, 5:13, youtube.com/watch?v=HdLOSztolZQ.

30. NewsOne Now, "More Sponsors Pull Ads From VH1's 'Sorority Sisters,' Is The Show Doomed?" Praise DC, December 19, 2014, praisedc.com/1723375/more-sponsors-pull-ads-from-vh1s-sorority-sisters-is-the-show-doomed.

31. "VH1 *Sorority Sisters*: The show was outrageous || STEVE HARVEY," interview with Steve Harvey, posted July 19, 2016, by Steve TV Show, YouTube, 3:04, youtube.com/watch?v=DRmg6ROdbSQ.

32. Treye Green, "DaBaby's HIV Rant—and Twitter Apology—Highlight Hip-Hop's LGBTQ Problem," NBC News, August 9, 2021, nbcnews.com /think/opinion/dababy-s-hiv-rant-twitter-apology-highlight-hip-hop-s -ncna1276215.

33. "Poppin," track 3 on Bizzle, *The Messenger 4: Independents Day*, God Over Money Records, 2020.

34. Leah Bitsky, "21 Savage Apologizes over 'Jewish Money' Lyric That Landed LeBron in Hot Water," *Page Six*, December 25, 2018, pagesix.com/2018/12 /25/21-savage-apologizes-over-jewish-money-lyric-that-landed-lebron-in -hot-water.

35. Saint Lauren Don (@21savage), "The Jewish people I know are very wise with there money so that's why I said we been gettin Jewish money . . . ," X, December 25, 2018, x.com/21savage/status/1077429256249061376.

36. Ronnie Tyler, "Wedding Video: Stephanie and Delano's Journey to Happily Ever After," Black and Married with Kids, October 2, 2012, blackandmarriedwithkids.com/wedding-video-stephanie-and-delanos -journey-to-happily-ever-after.

37. Howard Husock, "When Black Music Was Conservative: Songs from the Classic Soul Era Celebrated Marriage and Upward Mobility," *City Journal*, Summer 2015, city-journal.org/article/when-black-music-was -conservative.

Chapter Nine: Rally Marriage Advocates for Battle

1. Joy Jones, "'Marriage Is for White People'," *Washington Post*, March 25, 2006, washingtonpost.com/archive/opinions/2006/03/26/marriage-is-for-white -people/095b1136-1440-4380-ac23-64beeeac3df4.

2. Ibid.

3. Ibid.

4. Tera R. Hurt, "Black Men and the Decision to Marry," *Marriage and Family Review* 50, no. 6 (2014), doi:10.1080/01494929.2014.905816.

5. Ibid.

6. Andrew Lawrence, "Taking His Advice Was Like 'Chewing Broken Glass': The Short Life of Dating Guru Kevin Samuels," *Guardian*, May 13, 2022, theguardian.com/lifeandstyle/2022/may/13/relationship-guru-kevin -samuels-life-death.

7. "5 Qualities Black Men Look For in a Wife," BlackDoctor.org, accessed November 8, 2024, blackdoctor.org/qualities-men-want-in-a-wife.

8. Prv 12:4 (ESV).

9. Prv 21:9, 21:19 (ESV).

10. "Listen to Black Women - MASCULINE WOMEN," panel discussion, April 22. 2024, posted by MadameNoire, YouTube, 14:32, youtube.com /watch?v=Jik4xQyk3rQ. For my analysis, see Delano Squires (@DelanoSquires), "'Alpha females' have been imitating men," X, June 10, 2024, x.com/DelanoSquires/status/1800336670262485195.

11. Antonius D. Skipper et al., "Black Marriages Matter: Wisdom and Advice From Happily Married Black Couples," *Interdisciplinary Journal of Applied Family Science* 70 (2021): 1370, doi.org/10.1111/fare.12565.

12. Ibid.

13. Ibid., 1372.

14. Ibid.

15. "Are Black Women The Least Desired But Most Imitated? | Ask a Black Woman Ep. 2," panel discussion, September 6, 2017, posted by MadameNoire, YouTube, 9:37, youtube.com/watch?v=5T6PaCa6tB4.

16. Wendy Wang, "Who Cheats More? The Demographics of Infidelity in America," Institute for Family Studies, January 10, 2018, ifstudies.org /blog/who-cheats-more-the-demographics-of-cheating-in-america.

17. Ibid.

18. Ibid.

19. Nina Mandell, "NBA Players' Union Shows Players Being Dads in New Campaign," *USA Today*, June 2, 2015, ftw.usatoday.com/story/sports /nba/2015/06/02/nba-players-union-shows-players-being-dads-in-new -campaign/82082181007.

20. Diamonique Valentine, "As Hard As It May Be . . . ," Instagram, May 3, 2023, instagram.com/reel/CrwuFLxAVGK. For my analysis, see Delano Squires (@DelanoSquires), "One of the things that's lost when we unhitch marriage from family formation," X, May 4, 2023, x.com/DelanoSquires /status/1654317297761230849.

Index